AF413132

History of Prussia

*An Enthralling Overview of Major Events
and Figures in Prussian History*

Free limited time bonus

Stop for a moment. We have a free bonus set up for you. The problem is this: we forget 90% of everything that we read after 7 days. Crazy fact, right? Here's the solution: we've created a printable, 1-page pdf summary for this book that you're reading now. All you have to do to get your free pdf summary is to go to the following website: **https://livetolearn.lpages.co/enthrallinghistory/**

Or, Scan the QR code!

Once you do, it will be intuitive. Enjoy, and thank you!

Table of Contents

Introduction

Prussia no longer exists, but it is not an ancient nation. The memory of Prussia actually still lives vividly in the minds of many Germans, Poles, and Russians, and that memory is met with equal parts heartache, headache, and indifference. This book will explore the history of the land that would become Prussia, the people who inhabited it, and the dramatic collapse of this nation that was once among the most powerful in Europe.

Prussia's erasure from the map was so thorough that even its heartland has been absorbed into a different country entirely. The core of what was once Prussia is now the Kaliningrad Oblast, a Russian province separated from the rest of Russia by hundreds of miles and wedged between Lithuania, Poland, and the Baltic Sea. The city that was once Königsberg—Prussia's intellectual and cultural capital—is now Kaliningrad, and its streets are filled with Russian speakers rather than German ones. Germans maintain the strongest cultural memory of this land, but with Kaliningrad's overwhelmingly Russian population, any return to its former identity seems a distant dream. Prussia exists now only in history, in memory, and in the long shadow it casts across European politics.

Chapter 1: Origins and Foundations of Prussia

Baltic Tribes 1200 CE. [1]

The people who occupied the region that bore their name for the longest period were a group known as the "Old Prussians." These people spoke a common Baltic language, also known as Old Prussian, and were made up of several tribes, including the Sambians, Bartians, Nadruvians, and Pomesanians, among others. Their occupation of the land called Prussia and Brandenburg has been documented from the Iron Age (the 5ᵗʰ century BCE) until the Middle Ages. They worshiped pagan deities, which would eventually be used by others as the justification for conquering their land and converting them to Christianity.

The Romans knew of the Baltic tribes, whom they called the Aesti, meaning easterners, which was what their German neighbors called them. The Balts collected amber on the seashore, which was generally worthless to them but was worth more than gold to the Romans, who traded for it through German intermediaries. In exchange for amber, the Old Prussians received iron, weapons, Roman coins, and jewelry. Still, due to the long distance from the Baltic tribal lands to Rome, there is little Roman documentation about the details of how the Old Prussians lived. It is generally accepted that the Old Prussians were native to the area, but this, too, remains unknown for certain.

In the Early Middle Ages, more detailed descriptions of these people emerged. Legend says that the Old Prussians were brought together by a pair of brothers, Widewuto and Bruteno, who came from overseas. Widewuto was elected the *kriwe-kriwajto*, the highest leader among the Old Prussians and the intermediary between gods and men. He was obeyed by all the Baltic tribes; he would be similar to the pope of the Catholic Church. The other brother, Bruteno, instructed the people to worship the gods Patrimpas (god of spring and fertility), Perkūnas (god of thunder and justice), and Patulas (god of death). Images of these gods were placed in the trunk of an evergreen oak that grew in the holy place of Romuva, where the kriwe-kriwajto lived. The Old Prussian nobles would meet in this holy grove to make decisions on war and rule.

The Latvians were neighbors of the Old Prussians, and in Latvia, there is a place named Romuva, or the place of peace. It is believed that this was a common name for holy locations. In Romuva, no trees were cut down, no animals were hunted, and people could make sacrifices to the three high gods and possibly to the creator of everything, Deivs, who created the lesser gods and started the engine of the world.

The Old Prussians also worshiped a host of lesser gods, including a god of corn, a god of health, and *berzduki* and *markopoli*, which were house gnomes and spirits, respectively. Priests and priestesses were unmarried or widowed men and women who carried out religious rituals, including the sacrificing of animals, spoils of war, and, during hard periods, captives. They also blessed the land and dwellings and acted as teachers, soothsayers, and seers. Many of the priests lived with the kriwe-kriwajto in Romuva.

Legend says that when Bruteno and Widewuto reached a hundred years of age, they divided the land among Widewuto's sons. They told their people to remain peaceful and honor their gods, and then they climbed onto a funeral pyre in Romuva and sacrificed themselves for their people. The people elected a new kriwe-kriwajto from among their ranks.

According to Old Prussian beliefs, the brothers ascended to the world of the gods through fire. This was why the Old Prussians burned their dead, along with their weapons and tools, and why they sacrificed humans to appease the gods.

Bruteno and Widewuto were then worshiped as gods of farming, especially livestock. Stone images of the brothers were placed to mark the borders of various tribal lands. The Old Prussians remained true to their promise to the brothers, and the tribes remained peaceful with each other. When they were threatened, they banded together to fight off their common enemy.

The early history of the Old Prussians before the 10th century remains shrouded in mystery. We know they traded amber with the Romans through Germanic intermediaries and that this valuable trade brought them into contact—and likely conflict—with neighboring peoples. Later medieval chronicles and legends speak of ancient battles with Slavic tribes and invasions from all directions, but separating historical fact from folklore is nearly impossible with the limited sources available. What is clear is that by the time written records became more reliable in the late 10th century, the Old Prussians had established themselves as a fierce and independent people who would resist outside control for centuries to come.

The question of outside influences on Old Prussian culture remains debated among historians. From across the Baltic Sea came Scandinavian Vikings. The extent and nature of their presence in Prussia are not completely understood. Some historians, citing archaeological evidence from the Midgard Historical Center in Norway and the State Archaeological Museum in Warsaw, have argued that the Yotvingians (also called Sudovians), a people living in or near Old Prussian territory, were descended from Viking settlers who came from Scandinavia onto the Baltic coast in the 9th century. They point to burial practices that differed from those of the Old Prussians. The Yotvingians buried their dead near dwellings rather than cremating them. Swords with runic inscriptions have also been found in the Masurian Lake District. However, most modern scholars classify the Yotvingians as a separate Baltic tribe related to the Old Prussians rather than as descendants of Norse settlers. Whatever their origins, if Vikings did settle in significant numbers among the Baltic peoples, they never came to dominate the region. Viking raids in the Baltic were generally focused on plunder rather than conquest, and most raiders returned to Scandinavia or continued eastward to places like Kyiv (Kiev).

The first well-documented attempt to bring the Old Prussians under outside control came from the newly Christianized Kingdom of Poland. Mieszko I, the first Christian ruler of Poland, had unified various Slavic tribes under his rule in the late 10th century. His son, Bolesław I the Brave, became the first king of Poland. Along with expanding his kingdom, Bolesław also sought to convert the pagan Prussians by sending the missionary Adalbert, Bishop of Prague, in 997.

The details of Adalbert's mission come primarily from hagiographies (accounts of saints' lives written by Christians years after the events), so they must be treated with some caution. According to these accounts, Adalbert entered Prussian territory with only a small group of companions, including his half-brother Radim, a Pole named Benedict-Bogusza, and an interpreter. The Old Prussians, an oral society that relied heavily on face-to-face interactions, distrusted this stranger who read from books. In the first village where Adalbert preached, the bishop was reportedly struck on the head with an oar by a chieftain, and he and his companions were forced to flee. After being chased out of two more settlements, Adalbert and his group were set upon by an angry mob, possibly led by a local priest. The mob killed Adalbert and cut off his head. King Bolesław later bought Adalbert's remains from the Prussians for their weight in gold. Adalbert was subsequently made a saint in the Catholic Church, and tales about his martyrdom made Prussia more widely known in Christian Europe.

The failure of Adalbert's mission did not end the conflict between the Old Prussians and their Christian neighbors. The historical record for the next two centuries is fragmentary, but chronicles mention various clashes. In 1166, Henry, Duke of Sandomierz and a veteran of the Second Crusade, was killed in battle against the Prussians. Beyond such scattered references, we know little about the details of Polish-Prussian relations during this period. What is clear is that the Old Prussians maintained their independence and their pagan religion into the 13th century, despite the growing pressure from Christianized neighbors.

By the early 13th century, Polish rulers were making more concentrated efforts to subdue Prussia. The Kingdom of Poland had fractured into competing dukedoms, and one of these rulers, Konrad I, Duke of Masovia, sought to expand his territory northward into Prussian lands. His campaigns met with fierce resistance and Prussian counter-raids. Facing continued difficulty in conquering the region, Konrad made a fateful decision around 1226. He invited the Order of Brothers of the German House of Saint Mary, better known as the Teutonic Knights, to help defeat the Prussians. This invitation would change the course of Prussian history. The Teutonic Knights, a military-religious order that had fought in the Crusades in the Holy Land, brought their organizational skills, their military expertise, and the backing of the pope. Their arrival marked the beginning of a sustained and ultimately successful campaign to conquer and Christianize Prussia.

Chapter 2: The Teutonic Knights: Prussia's Medieval Crusaders

The story of the Teutonic Knights might not have captured the public imagination like other orders, such as the Templars, but its story is certainly cinematic in scope. The Teutonic Knights were late arrivals among the medieval military orders. By the time they were founded in 1190, the Knights Templar and the Knights Hospitaller had already established themselves as powerful forces in the Crusader States. The Teutonic Order originated during the siege of Acre, when German merchants from the towns of Bremen and Lübeck established a field hospital for their sick and wounded countrymen. The German crusaders were attempting to recapture the city of Acre, an incredibly important port on the coast of the Levant. King Guy of Jerusalem granted the German merchants a plot of land and a street in Acre once the city was taken. The Germans prevailed, and the hospital was established in the newly conquered city.

The hospital was recognized as a religious fraternity by Pope Celestine III in 1196, and in 1198, it was formally transformed into a military order. It was officially called the Brothers of the Hospital of St. Mary of the German Nation. The name "Teutonic" comes from the Latin phrase "of the Germans," *Theutonicorum*, which itself derives from the Teutones, an ancient Germanic tribe. Unlike the older military orders whose leadership had long been established, the Teutonic Order's first grand master was Heinrich Walpot von Bassenheim, a Rhenish knight from a noble family. He led the order from 1198 until his death around 1200.

From its inception as a military order, the Teutonic Knights required their knight-brothers to be of noble or knightly origin, following the model of the Templars and Hospitallers. The knights were first and foremost dedicated to Jesus Christ and were exempt from secular justice. They were abstinent and renounced their personal property and free will once they joined. Living arrangements were simple, and meals were shared. Like the Templars, they wore a white mantle, but theirs bore a large black cross instead of a red one. They were to live by strict rules of behavior that produced chaste, humble, obedient, and charitable men. They were, in essence, warrior monks. They were led by a grand master, who was elected by a council of thirteen, who were in turn elected by officials within the organization.

The order was not just knights and monks. It also consisted of laymen who were employed as workers, warriors, and knights' retainers. They wore only a white mantle with no cross. The members of the order came from various backgrounds. While most were German, some were Polish and Slavic.

The Teutonic Order existed mostly on the periphery of the Crusader States until the reign of Frederick II, who was crowned Holy Roman emperor in 1220. One of Frederick's chief advisors was Hermann von Salza, the fourth grand master of the Teutonic Knights. Under Salza's leadership and through his political connections, the Teutonic Order received recognition equal to the Knights Hospitaller and the Knights Templar. Pope Honorius III and his admiration for Salza helped the order rise in prominence.

Salza's origins are unclear, but it seems he was descended from a family of ministeriales (unfree nobles who made up much of the German knighthood in the High Middle Ages). The ministeriales formed a unique place in German society, as they were of high birth but not considered freemen, a requirement for many organizations. Salza had possibly been part of the Fifth Crusade, and either there or during the Sixth Crusade, he formed his bond with Frederick. He most likely helped to arrange for the emperor's marriage to Isabella, the princess of Jerusalem, and the eventual sidelining of Isabella's father, the king of Jerusalem. Frederick then took the title of king of Jerusalem, though this was disputed at the time for several reasons, not least of which was the fact that he had been twice excommunicated and could not, therefore, legally be on a crusade.

Upon returning to Europe, Frederick and Hermann von Salza took part in the War of the Keys, which was the first military action taken by a pope against one of Europe's royal houses. It is not clear if Salza or the Teutonic Knights fought in the war. However, peace negotiations were resolved through the intervention of the grand master and several German princes. Frederick's excommunication was finally lifted in 1230.

Before this, the order had already embarked on its first major military venture outside the Holy Land. In 1211, King Andrew II of Hungary invited the Teutonic Knights to the region of Burzenland in southeastern Transylvania to defend against incursions by the nomadic Cumans. The order built five castles in the region and settled German colonists there. However, as the knights grew more powerful and autonomous, Hungarian nobles became alarmed. When the Teutonic Knights attempted to place themselves directly under papal authority rather than that of the Hungarian crown in 1224, King Andrew responded by expelling them from Transylvania in 1225, though he allowed the German settlers to remain.

After this setback, Duke Konrad I of Masovia contacted Hermann von Salza and asked for support from the Teutonic Knights in conquering and converting the Old Prussians in what would be known as the "Prussian Crusade." Konrad's offer was even more enticing than King Andrew's had been because the duke of Masovia promised the order that for their efforts in converting the pagan Prussians, they would be rewarded with territories along the Vistula River. Salza realized the opportunity that this presented. Emperor Frederick approved the plan, so Salza approached the pope, resulting in the Golden Bull of Rimini of 1226. This established that the territories granted to the order would be sovereign, and it made the grand master a prince of the Holy Roman Empire. The order would also be free from all imperial "taxes, burdens, and services."

The other missionary force in Prussia, the Cistercian monks, became allies to the Teutonic Knights, and the two orders became pillars of this new crusade. While the Old Prussians had held off previous attempts at conquest, by the 1230s, their territory was already being threatened by the slow encroachment of Christian German settlers from the south and west. German settlements were springing up all along the Baltic coast. The Teutonic Knights were once again late to the scene. While their numbers were few to begin with, they had something the Old Prussians lacked and something the German settlers needed: order, organization, and coordination. Salza recognized the significance of this new crusade. As the age of chivalric warfare was beginning to evolve, the Teutonic Knights were securing for themselves a clear legacy in the form of a new state.

By 1230, the order had established itself around Kulm and Lübau, and Duke Konrad had handed these lands over to them. To avoid becoming a pawn between the empire and the papacy, Salza had the pope declare the land the property of Saint Peter. However, it was not long before the Polish nobility, including the duke, began to consider the order an unwelcome intruder. The order's position was not initially strong militarily or financially. They were assisted by land grants on the island of Sicily by Frederick, who had taken them from the Templars and the Order of St. John. Additionally, their numbers began to increase as the crusade attracted German warriors and knights seeking spiritual merit. Most of the actual fighting was done by German crusaders who were not members of the order itself. Since this was a crusade sanctioned by Rome, participants could have their sins forgiven.

The order pushed east across the Vistula, building castles as they went. The local Prussian tribes seemed hindered by internal conflicts and unable to mount a unified resistance initially. In 1239, Hermann von Salza died, never having set foot in the nation he was creating. In 1255, Otakar, King of Bohemia, joined the crusade. In Samland, they built a new fortress named Königsberg, which bore on its coat of arms a knight with a crowned helm.

Unlike the crusades in the Holy Land, the campaign in Prussia was focused on creating a permanent Christian state through military conquest and colonization. The Teutonic Order's official mission was to convert the pagan Prussians to Christianity; this was their papal mandate and crusading justification. In practice, however, the campaign relied heavily on military force rather than peaceful conversion. The Teutonic Order conducted mass forced baptisms under armed supervision, destroyed pagan shrines, and suppressed traditional Prussian religious practices.

Tensions emerged between the Teutonic Order's stated religious mission and the political reality. While the Treaty of Christburg in 1249 promised civil liberties to Prussian converts, these rights were often not honored, particularly after the major uprisings that started in 1260. As a minority ruling over a conquered population, the German knights maintained control through military superiority and a feudal system that kept most Prussians subordinate regardless of their religious status. The conquest was marked by brutal suppression. Prussians who resisted conversion were killed, enslaved, or driven into exile, while those who converted found themselves under the tight control of a foreign military order.

Obviously, the conquest was far from smooth. The Old Prussians mounted fierce resistance, and the campaign was marked by numerous setbacks and revolts. Major uprisings erupted around 1260 and continued for over a decade. The Prussians proved to be formidable opponents, and it took the order decades of sustained military effort to subdue them. When the Teutonic Order finally suppressed the last major resistance in the early 1280s, they demanded complete subjugation. Prussian nobles were placed under feudal obligations that stripped away any remaining independence.

At the same time, successive waves of German immigrants led to the gradual Germanization of Prussia. The German language became increasingly dominant. Christianity spread, and by the 14th century, there was little left of the Old Prussians as a distinct people. Prussia had, in many ways, become a German territory under the rule of the Teutonic Order.

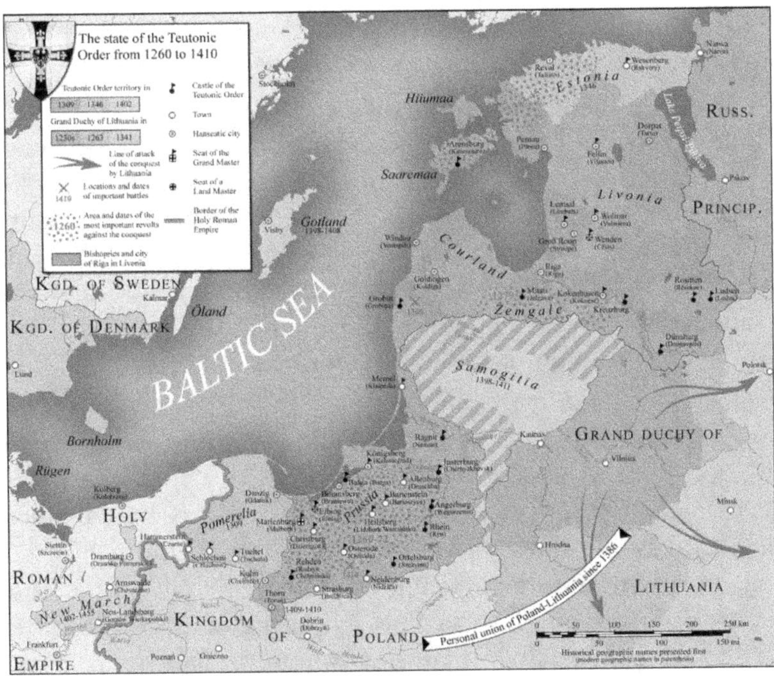

The spread of the Teutonic Order from 1230 to 1410.[*]

After the conquest and subjugation of Prussia, the order turned its sights to the lands to the west of the Vistula: Polish-owned Pomerelia (a sub-region of Pomerania). Standing in their way were the margraves of Brandenburg, who considered themselves the heirs of Pomerelia. They swooped in to occupy the city of Danzig. King Vladislav of Poland called on the Teutonic Knights to expel the Brandenburgers, which the order completed in 1308. The order then demanded a payment that the king could not afford, but it declared that it would be content to keep Danzig and the rest of Pomerelia. At the same time, they paid off the Brandenburgers to renounce their claim to the land. The order now controlled the Vistula estuary and would eventually connect their territory to the rest of the empire.

Yet, their expansion was curbed by a new alliance between the Poles and the "heathen" Lithuanians whose rule extended from the Baltic to Kiev. Through marriage and the forced conversion of the Lithuanians, the union between them and the Poles was not just a barrier to Teutonic expansion but a threat to the continued survival of Prussia as a Germanic state. To push back against their neighbors' aggression, Grand Master Ulrich von Jungingen assembled a large army for a decisive confrontation. Contemporary sources provide varying estimates of the forces involved at the Battle of Grunwald in 1410, with the Teutonic army likely numbering between twenty thousand and twenty-seven thousand men, including knights, mercenaries, and auxiliaries.

Jungingen gambled everything on this battle. The Teutonic forces were soundly defeated, not just by the size of the Polish-Lithuanian army but also by superior tactics. Grand Master von Jungingen was killed in the fighting, along with most of the Teutonic Order's leadership. The Teutonic Order survived, though, by successfully defending its capital at Malbork Castle during the subsequent siege. After several weeks, the Polish-Lithuanian forces lifted the siege, and the Peace of Toruń was signed in 1411, though it required substantial reparations from the Teutonic Order.

The new grand master, Heinrich von Plauen, was more content with consolidation than expansion, but eventually, his hand was forced. The landed nobility of Prussia, composed mainly of those descended from German immigrants, had grown to dislike the Teutonic Order. The Peace of Toruń required large payments to Poland, which the order could only raise through heavy taxation. Internal conflict within the order got out of control. King Vladislav allowed bands of Poles and Lithuanians to raid the Prussian borderlands.

Grand Master von Plauen failed to receive help from Hungary, so he attempted to take the fight to the Poles. However, he was met with failure, largely due to the divisions within the order. In 1440, the Prussian nobility founded the Prussian League, which formed an alternative government that eventually opposed the order. They looked for protection from their strongest neighbor, Poland.

The result was the Second Peace of Toruń of 1466, which declared that the western territories of the Teutonic Order's state, including Pomerelia and the city of Gdańsk, would be ceded to Poland as Royal Prussia. The Teutonic Order retained control of eastern Prussia, but it was now a fief of the Polish crown, so the grand master had to swear fealty to the king of Poland.

As a show of defiance, the order elected grand masters with strong German backgrounds. In 1511, the grand master was Margrave Albert of Brandenburg-Ansbach. Under him, the order became a secular institution, and Prussia became a secular state. The black cross disappeared from the mantle and shield. The Teutonic Order was essentially over.

The order undoubtedly played a major role in the formation of the Prussian state. While the Teutonic Knights brought administrative structures modeled on the Holy Roman Empire and established an economic system based on large-scale agriculture, their rule came at a tremendous cost to the native Old Prussians. The conquest involved decades of brutal warfare, forced conversions, and the systematic suppression of Prussian culture and religion. Many Old Prussians were killed, exiled, or reduced to serfdom, particularly after the major uprisings of the 1260s–1280s. Those who remained were gradually assimilated through Germanization, a process the Teutonic Order accelerated but did not start.

By the 14th century, the distinct Old Prussian language and culture were fading, replaced by the German language, law, and customs. While some Prussian nobles who submitted to the Teutonic Order retained certain privileges, and some Prussians served as auxiliaries or converts within the new society, the relationship was fundamentally one of conquest and domination rather than partnership. The Teutonic Order's legacy in Prussia is a complex one. They established systems of governance and agriculture that would shape the region's future, but this development was built upon the subjugation and cultural erasure of the indigenous population.

Chapter 3: The Margraviate of Brandenburg and the Hohenzollern Dynasty

A margrave is a German nobleman who ranks above a count. Margraves in the 14th and 15th centuries were princes of the Holy Roman Empire. The Margraviate of Brandenburg began in the Northern March (Nordmark). This area is equivalent to the modern German state of Brandenburg, located in the northeast of the country.

The first margrave in that region is believed to have been Gero I in 937, though he was not the margrave of Brandenburg. Gero expanded his originally modest holdings into the vast territory called Marca Geronis or March of Gero, which was considered a super-march. The Slavic rebellion of 983 disrupted the power dynamics of the region for some time, and the area was largely under the control of the Slavic Lutici alliance, which fell in the middle of the 11th century. The rule was somewhat restored by Prince Pribislav-Henry, a Slavic-Christian prince and the last ruler of the Hevelli tribe (a Slavic tribe) in the Nordmark. Pribislav, upon his death in 1150, left the territory to the House of Ascania, an Old Saxon noble family.

Albert the Bear of Ascania declared himself the margrave of Brandenburg, thus firmly establishing his march, which he expanded through crusades against the nearby Slavic Wend tribes. The Margraviate of Brandenburg, controlled by the House of Ascania, was officially established in 1157. Albert accompanied Emperor Frederick Barbossa in his campaign in Italy, distinguishing himself in the taking of Milan. When Albert died in 1164, he divided his territory between his six sons.

The Margraviate of Brandenburg passed to his eldest son, Otto, whose godfather had been none other than Prince Pribislav. Otto married Judith, a member of the House of Piast, the ruling family of Poland. She was the sister of Boleslaw IV and Mieszko III, both dukes of Poland. Otto did not expand his territory and instead focused on stabilizing the region. The Margraviate of Brandenburg, at that time, did not correspond to the current state of Brandenburg; it was the eastern land of the River Havel and the Zauche Plateau to the south. In Zauche, Otto founded the Lehnin Abbey, which remains a part of Brandenburg to this day.

When Otto I died in 1184, his eldest son, Otto II, took over the margraviate. From 1198 to 1199, Otto II devastated the Danish in Pomerania and consolidated his power to the east. He supported Philip of Swabia as king of Germany until Otto's death in 1205. He did not leave an heir from his marriage to Ada of Holland, his father's widow and his stepmother. The margraviate then passed to his younger brother and stepson, Albert II, the youngest son of Otto I and Ada of Holland.

Albert had joined the German Crusade of 1197 and was present in the Holy Land for the founding of the Teutonic Order. After Albert took over as margrave of Brandenburg, Philip of Swabia was assassinated in 1208. He had supported Philip, but after his death, he supported Philip's adversary, Holy Roman Emperor Otto IV. Albert secured areas like Teltow, Prignitz, and parts of the Uckermark, but lost Pomerania to the House of Griffin. When Albert died in 1220, his sons, John I and Otto III, ruled jointly as margraves. The brothers expanded the margraviate and died a year apart in 1266 and 1267.

The margraves of Brandenburg's relationship with Prussia and the ruling Teutonic Order at the time was complicated, to say the least. Many members of the House of Ascania joined the order and fought to secure Prussia, but there was also conflict between the rulers of Brandenburg and Prussia. The territory of Pomerelia remained an area of conflict for many years. It had been Christianized, and in 1217, the ruler of Gdańsk, Swietopelk II, declared himself the duke of Pomerelia. A civil war erupted between him and his brothers, with one side siding with the Teutonic Knights and Swietopelk allying with the Old Prussians, who revolted against the Teutonic Order in 1242. When Swietopelk died in 1266, his dukedom passed to his sons, who began another civil war. One son, Mestwin II, allied himself with the margraves of Brandenburg, the co-rulers John II, Otto IV, and Conrad I, who were all sons of John I. The longest-lived and most well-known of these was Otto IV, known as "with the arrow" because he lived for about a year with an arrow sticking out of his head.

The Brandenburgers were allowed, per the provisions of a treaty signed between them and Mestwin II, to keep troops within Pomerelia for a certain amount of time while Mestwin battled his brother and uncle for supremacy. Once the time was up and Mestwin had established himself as the sole ruler of Pomerelia, the Brandenburgers refused to remove their troops. This led to a conflict between the previous allies, which resulted in Mestwin calling for help from Poland.

Pomerelia became a fief of Poland, but after Mestwin's death and an attempted Polish takeover, the Ascanians made their move to take Pomerelia. In the struggle, the Teutonic Order took control of Danzig in 1308. The exact circumstances of this takeover, including the degree of violence, negotiations, and the ultimate treaty arrangements through which Brandenburg relinquished its claims, remain debated among historians, though it is clear that the Teutonic Order eventually secured the city through a combination of force and diplomacy.

In this same year, Waldemar the Great of the House of Ascania came into power in Brandenburg. Waldemar secured the rest of Pomerelia for Brandenburg, but he relinquished his claim to all lands east of the River Leba in 1309 to the Teutonic Order. Waldemar died childless, and the margraviate fell to the young Henry II, his cousin, who was the last margrave of Brandenburg from the House of Ascania.

Henry II only lived for about a year after becoming the margrave. Brandenburg passed to the House of Wittelsbach, and the new margrave was Louis V, called "the Brandenburger." He ruled as the margrave of Brandenburg from 1323 to 1351 and the duke of Bavaria from 1347 to 1361. Louis was the son of Louis IV, the Holy Roman emperor.

Louis V was not of age to rule when he became margrave. His regent was Berthold VII, Count of Henneberg. One distantly related member of the Ascanian family, Rudolf I, Duke of Saxe-Wittenberg, had to be bought off to renounce his claim to the margraviate. When Louis came of age, he married Princess Margaret, daughter of King Christopher II of Denmark, to strengthen the standing of the Wittelsbach dynasty.

However, Louis was never very popular in Brandenburg. Civil unrest eventually created another Brandenburg-Pomeranian war, part of a series of conflicts that lasted from the 13th century until 1637, when the House of Griffin (also known as the House of Pomerania) died out. The Pomeranians were forced to abandon the Uckermark after suffering defeats, but they were able to avoid Brandenburg's dominance by becoming a papal fief in 1330.

In 1336, Louis joined the Teutonic Knights in the Lithuanian Crusade. The Lithuanians, led by Duke Margiris, are remembered for their valiant last stand at the hill fort of Pilėnai, the location of which remains unknown to scholars. According to later accounts, some of which historians have identified as embellished, some four thousand people sheltering at the fort committed mass suicide in a tragic and dramatic act of defiance that continues to inspire Lithuanians to this day. In 1338, Louis concluded a peace with the Lithuanians in which he gave up any ownership of the land but retained rights of succession.

Louis naturally sided with his father in a political standoff with Pope Benedict XII. He backed his brother-in-law, Valdemar IV, as king of Denmark, which strengthened relations with the Danish court even after Louis's wife died in 1340. From that point onward, he spent most of his time in Bavaria and Tyrol. In 1342, he married the Tyrolean countess, Margaret, even though she was not technically divorced from her previous husband, a Luxembourg prince named John Henry.

Louis, through his paternal grandmother's line, was of the House of Habsburg as well as the House of Wittelsbach. The Habsburgs and Luxembourg were often rivals in the dynastic struggles of Europe. However, Louis's father, Louis IV, was considered the safest choice for Holy Roman emperor over Fredrick the Fair of the House of Habsburg. When Countess Margaret expelled her husband, John Henry, from Tyrol, Emperor Louis supported her claim that their marriage had not been consummated and pushed his newly widowed son, Louis V, to marry Margaret to add her lands to the expanding lands of the House of Wittelsbach. The newest pope, Pope Clement VI, however, excommunicated the couple even though the emperor had employed two well-regarded scholars to support his cause. Regardless, Louis's marriage went through.

In 1347, Holy Roman Emperor Louis IV died. Louis V succeeded him as duke of Bavaria. However, he was not selected to be the next emperor; this role went to Charles IV of Bohemia and the House of

Luxembourg. Charles also happened to be the elder brother of Louis's wife's ex-husband, John Henry.

The House of Wittelsbach elected Günther von Schwarzburg as the anti-king of Germany. Though this attempted overthrow failed, it led to several years of strife between Charles and Louis, which erupted into war. After losing much of Brandenburg and repelling an attack on Tyrol, Louis V was faced with civil unrest after the appearance of a "false Waldemar," who claimed to be the dead Waldemar, Margrave of Brandenburg from the House of Ascania. This was likely a ploy by Charles to undermine Louis's power, but it did not work. Peace was finally reached between the two sides in 1350, when the Wittelsbachs regained Brandenburg and retained all their other possessions. The margraviate of Brandenburg was then given to two of Louis's brothers, Louis VI the Roman and Otto V the Bavarian.

When Louis the Roman first took over Brandenburg, the "False Waldemar" was still causing trouble within the margraviate. However, with the peace with the emperor, this was quickly stamped out. Louis the Roman was married to Princess Cunigunde, daughter of Casimir III, King of Poland. Through this marriage, he hoped to gain the Polish crown when the king died, but his wife died first. Louis then married Ingeborg of Mecklenburg, daughter of the duke of Mecklenburg.

The Golden Bull of 1356 made Brandenburg an electorate, meaning that the margrave would be a member of the electoral college that selected the next Holy Roman emperor. About a decade later, in 1365, Louis the Roman died without an heir in Berlin. The Electorate of Brandenburg then passed to his brother, Otto V.

In 1366, Otto married Catherine of Bohemia, daughter of Holy Roman Emperor Charles IV, a member of the House of Luxembourg. Twenty-four-year-old Catherine was already a widow. She had been married to Rudolf of Austria for nine years. Otto promised his father-in-law the power of succession in Brandenburg upon his death.

After becoming sole elector in 1365, Otto spent extended periods at the court of his father-in-law in Bohemia rather than governing his own territory. He even handed Brandenburg's administration to Charles IV for six years, essentially allowing the emperor to run the margraviate while Otto remained the nominal ruler.

Financially, Otto's rule was disastrous. He sold Lower Lusatia, which he had already pledged to the Wettin dynasty, to Charles IV in 1367, trading away Brandenburg territory for quick cash. He renewed old border disputes with Poland and turned a brief friendship with Pomeranian dukes into renewed hostility.

By 1371, Otto's financial situation had become so bad that he could not mount an effective defense of Brandenburg. Charles IV had successfully isolated him by winning over potential allies. When Charles invaded in 1371, Otto had neither the money, the army, nor the political support to resist. Otto resigned from the electorate in exchange for a large monetary compensation and retired to Bavaria. Otto V was the end of the Wittelsbach dynasty in Brandenburg.

The House of Luxembourg now controlled the electorate. The emperor placed his son, Wenceslaus, in the seat of power. The prince was twelve years old and had already been the king of Bohemia for ten years. Historically, the young boy is known as Wenceslaus IV of Bohemia. Born in 1361, Wenceslaus was the son of Emperor Charles IV and his third wife, Anna von Schweidnitz, a member of the Polish Piast royal family. Though Charles IV had a higher regard for his heritage along his mother's line, through his father, he was a scion of the House of Luxembourg, which included Holy Roman Emperor Henry VII.

When Charles died in 1378, Wenceslaus was just seventeen years old. He became his father's heir to both the Kingdom of Germany and the Holy Roman Empire. However, his hold on those governments was often tenuous, and he faced many challenges to his rule.

Upon Charles's death, Brandenburg went to Wenceslaus's younger half-brother, Sigismund, who was just ten years old. Sigismund eventually became more focused on his role as the king of Hungary, so he gave the Electorate of Brandenburg to his cousin, Jobst of Moravia. Six years later, Jobst joined a rebellion of nobles against Wenceslaus, who had been unable to secure the imperial crown and was barely hanging on to the German one. In 1400, Wenceslaus was removed from the throne, and Rupert of the House of Wittelsbach became the new king of Germany (a role also known as the "King of the Romans").

When Rupert died in 1410, there was a period of tension, with Jobst, Sigismund, and Wenceslaus all vying for the throne. However, Jobst died in 1411, and Wenceslaus agreed to give up the German throne in exchange for remaining king of Bohemia. Sigismund became not only king of Hungary and Germany, but he also became the Holy Roman emperor in 1433. In exchange for supporting Sigismund in his bid for the throne, Frederick VI of the House of Hohenzollern became the new elector of Brandenburg.

The Hohenzollern family originated in the Swabia region of southern Germany. Their center was originally Hohenzollern Castle on Mount Hohenzollern in the Swabian Alps. The family is mentioned in historical documents that date back to the 11th century. Frederick III, Count of Zollern, became Frederick I, Burgrave of Nuremberg, in 1192. The burgraviate remained in the Zollern family for over two centuries, passing through several generations until Frederick VI, Burgrave of Nuremberg, became Frederick I, Elector of Brandenburg, in 1415.

Frederick was born in Nuremberg in 1371 and fought alongside Sigismund against Ottoman forces in 1395. When Frederick's father died, he co-ruled Nuremberg with his brother, John, and also inherited the Principality of Ansbach. After supporting Sigismund and receiving Brandenburg, Frederick fought against the unruly nobles of Brandenburg to secure his authority. Frederick moved the capital of Brandenburg to Berlin.

Eventually, Frederick tired of his duties and passed on the role of margrave to his son, John, in 1426, though he kept the electorate title for himself. John, called "the Alchemist," was not particularly interested in governance, and his rule was largely ineffectual. He spent most of his time trying to turn ordinary materials into gold, hence his nickname. In 1427, Frederick persuaded John to take the mineral-rich lands of Bayreuth. Eventually, he handed over the administration of Brandenburg to John's younger brother, Frederick II, nicknamed "the Iron."

Frederick II focused his attention on pacifying the restless nobles of Brandenburg and avoided imperial politics. In 1440, Frederick I died, and Frederick II became elector in his own right while John the Alchemist retired to pursue his passion. In that same year, tensions rose when Frederick II announced his plans to build a residence on the Cölln island in the Spree River next to Berlin. This meant that parts of the city would be forcibly obtained by the electorate at the loss of the city.

In 1448, this spilled over into open revolt when citizens poured into the excavated land of what would become the Stadtschloss or the Berlin Palace. This palace would be the seat of the electors of Brandenburg, kings of Prussia, and German emperors in future centuries. In the mid-

15th century, Frederick called in his troops. The rebellion was stopped, and construction continued. In 1454 and 1455, Frederick concluded the Treaties of Cölln and Mewe, in which he secured the Neumark (New March), which had previously been lost to the Teutonic Order, for the Electorate of Brandenburg. In 1470, Frederick abdicated in favor of his younger brother, Albrecht Achilles, and retired to the principality of Bayreuth, where he died a year later.

Albrecht III Achilles was the third son of Frederick I and the fourth margrave of Brandenburg from the House of Hohenzollern. The imperial crown was now securely in the hands of the Habsburgs. Albrecht had fought alongside Holy Roman Emperor Albert II in his war against the Hussites, an early Protestant group formed by Jan Hus. Albrecht was a member of the Order of the Swan, a knightly order formed by Frederick II and based on the medieval tale of the Swan Knight. As a knight, Albrecht was known for being virtuous and skilled. He gained the nickname "Achilles" after the great Greek warrior of legend.

After Frederick I's death in 1440, Albrecht was given the Principality of Ansbach. He attempted to expand his territory by various means but was largely unsuccessful. After the abdication of his brother Frederick II, he gained control of all the Hohenzollern lands, the most important being the Electorate of Brandenburg. After a war with Pomerania, he secured the Duchy of Pomerania as part of Brandenburg. In 1486, he handed control over Brandenburg to his eldest son, John Cicero.

John established the Berlin Palace as the permanent residence of the elector of Brandenburg, thus making Berlin the capital. When he died in 1499, he was the first member of the House of Hohenzollern to be buried in Brandenburg. His son, Joachim I Nestor, became elector after his death. Joachim proved to be a firm but sensible ruler. He established order through stern measures, improved the administration of justice, encouraged commerce, and listened to the needs of the growing towns in his domain. In 1519, after the death of Holy Roman Emperor Maximilian I, Joachim's electoral vote was highly sought after by the two rivals for the throne of the Holy Roman Empire, Francis I of France and Charles of Burgundy (King of Spain). Joachim backed the winning Charles, who became Emperor Charles V, though relations between the elector of Brandenburg and the emperor were fairly cool.

Joachim was able to secure the Electorate of Mainz for his brother Albert, which gave the House of Hohenzollern two of the seven electoral votes to approve the Holy Roman emperor. The bribery needed to obtain this position was significant. To pay off his debts, Albert was given papal authority to sell indulgences to his parishioners. As a result, Albert became the focus of Martin Luther's sermons in nearby Saxony. Joachim was a great supporter of the Roman Catholic Church, and the Hohenzollerns were, at that point, opposed to the Reformation movements within the church. Yet he could not stop the tide of the Protestant movement. His wife, Elizabeth of Denmark, converted to Lutheranism and fled to Saxony.

While Joachim struggled with the Reformation in Brandenburg, his cousin faced an even more dramatic transformation far to the east. Albert of Brandenburg-Ansbach, from a cadet branch of the Hohenzollern family, had been elected grand master of the Teutonic Knights in 1511. The military order that had once been the scourge of the pagans now found itself in dire straits. Decades of warfare with Poland had drained its coffers and reduced its territory. The Second Peace of Thorn in 1466 had left the Teutonic Order's remaining lands (the region around Königsberg in East Prussia) as a fief of the Polish crown. The Teutonic Order owed fealty to the very kingdom it had once sought to conquer.

By the 1520s, the Teutonic Order was sinking under a mountain of debt estimated at over 200,000 gulden. Its very purpose—crusading against pagans—had become obsolete. The Reformation offered Albert an escape from this dying institution. In 1522 and 1523, he traveled to Wittenberg and Nuremberg to consult with Martin Luther and other Protestant reformers. Luther's advice was radical: dissolve the Teutonic Order, convert to Lutheranism, and transform the monastic state into a hereditary secular duchy.

Albert took Luther's counsel to heart. After securing the support of the Prussian estates and local knights who were weary of the Teutonic Order's papal ties and mounting debts, Albert made his move. On February 10th, 1525, he resigned his position as grand master, formally converted to Lutheranism, and proclaimed the dissolution of the Teutonic Order in Prussia. The transformation required legitimacy, which only the Polish king could provide. Negotiations with King Sigismund I of Poland culminated in the Treaty of Kraków, which was signed on April 8th, 1525. Two days later, on April 10th, Albert knelt before the Polish king in Kraków's market square and paid homage, becoming Albert, Duke of Prussia. He was the first duke of a new secular state.

The Duchy of Prussia had been born, and it was unlike anything Europe had seen before. It was the first Protestant state, and it had been created through the abandonment of monastic vows and the secularization of church lands. Albert could now marry, establish a dynasty, and rule as a secular prince. The transformation did not bring radical social change. The former commanders of the Teutonic Order simply converted to Lutheranism and retained their positions in the social hierarchy. However, it fundamentally altered the political landscape of northeastern Europe. Prussia was no longer a crusading order answerable to the pope but a hereditary duchy answerable to Poland.

The new duchy remained a Polish fief, requiring Albert and his successors to pay homage to the Polish crown and provide military support when called upon. This vassalage would endure for over a century, something that rankled future Hohenzollern rulers who dreamed of sovereignty.

Joachim died in 1535, still a stalwart Catholic. He never reconciled with his Protestant wife and seemed unaware of just how momentous his cousin's actions in faraway Prussia would prove for the future of their house.

His eldest son, Joachim II Hector, became the elector of Brandenburg. Joachim II had been forced by his father to sign a document promising to remain a Roman Catholic so he could remain heir to Brandenburg. However, after his father's death, Joachim II began to turn toward Protestantism. He did not openly convert until Charles V abdicated his throne and his brother, Ferdinand I, became the new Holy Roman emperor.

Previously, a pogrom in Brandenburg had forced Jewish citizens to flee the region. Under Joachim II, they were allowed to return after the Jewish advocate Josel of Rosheim pleaded their case directly to him. Joachim II spent lavishly, indulging in various passions to the point that he racked up a debt of 600,000 thalers by 1540. He tried to pay off his debt by confiscating church property and raising taxes.

In 1541, Joachim II joined Holy Roman Emperor Ferdinand in battling the Turks as they pressed into eastern Europe. He participated in the Siege of Buda, the capital of the Kingdom of Hungary. However, he was defeated and then defeated again in the Siege of Pest in the following year. Joachim II died in 1571. By that time, the Duchy of Prussia had already passed to Albert Frederick, who was a member of the Ansbach branch of the Hohenzollern family.

John George, Joachim II's eldest son, inherited the Electorate of Brandenburg, as well as a large amount of debt. He raised the grain tax, which heavily burdened the common people while the nobles—particularly the landed Junkers of Brandenburg's rural estates—were largely exempt. These Junker families, the estate-owning nobility east of the Elbe, controlled vast grain-producing lands worked by peasant labor and jealously guarded their tax exemptions and other feudal privileges.

John George once again banished the Jews from Brandenburg. A staunch Lutheran, he did allow Calvinist refugees from the Netherlands to enter his domain. In 1577, possibly because Duke Albert Frederick was exhibiting signs of mental illness, John George became co-regent of Prussia. He died in 1598, leaving Brandenburg to his son, Joachim Frederick, who reigned for ten years. The electorate then passed to Joachim Frederick's son, John Sigismund, in 1608.

When Duke Albert Frederick of Prussia died in 1618, John Sigismund was declared the new duke of Prussia by the Polish king. Brandenburg and Prussia were now combined. They had separate administrations, but both were ruled by John Sigismund of the House of Hohenzollern. John Sigismund was born Lutheran, but he converted to Calvinism. Because most of his subjects were Lutheran or Roman Catholic, he had initially drawn up plans of mass conversions within both regions, but he faced protests, particularly from his wife, who was a devout Lutheran. John Sigismund suffered a stroke and died in 1619.

His successor and son was George William. He was born in Cölln in 1595 to the elector of Brandenburg and his wife, Anna of Prussia. George William's mother was the daughter of Duke Albert Frederick, so he was truly the direct male heir to both Brandenburg and Prussia. George William married Elizabeth Charlotte of the Palatinate (a region in today's southern Germany). They had one son and two daughters.

George William proved to be an ineffective leader. This was not helped by the eruption of the Thirty Years' War in 1618, which broke out just before he became elector and duke. He tried to remain neutral in the fight between Holy Roman Emperor Ferdinand II and his

Lutheran opponents, but the war entered his territory anyway, leading to widespread looting by Catholic forces. When George's brother-in-law, Gustavus Adolphus of Sweden, intervened in the war, George reluctantly aligned with him. However, despite their ties, Swedish-Protestant troops still plundered parts of Brandenburg. After Gustavus was killed, George William withdrew from the war, leaving the government in the hands of a subordinate. He died in 1640 and was succeeded by his son, Frederick William.

Chapter 4: The Great Elector, Frederick William

Frederick William was twenty years old when he succeeded to the throne. He had hardly any experience in government or administration. He had grown up with a deep admiration of Gustavus Adolphus. Frederick William was educated in Küstrin instead of Berlin due to the Thirty Years' War, which had caused a lot of devastation to Brandenburg and Prussia. In 1634, he traveled to the Netherlands and studied mathematics, Latin, history, and warfare in Leyden. He spoke German, French, Dutch, and Polish. Frederick William grew to sympathize with the Dutch and the House

Frederick William, the Great Elector of Brandenburg and Duke of Prussia.'

of Orange's struggle against the Catholics, the Spanish, and the House of Habsburg.

When his father decided Brandenburg should fight the Swedes and join the Habsburgs' side of the war, Frederick found himself in opposition to his father and his father's powerful advisor, Adam, Count of Schwarzenberg. Frederick was effectively banished from his father's court and political life in general. When Elector George William died, Brandenburg and the House of Hohenzollern were at an all-time low. The most important holdings, economically speaking, were in Prussia, where the duke of Prussia, thanks to the Teutonic Order's consolidations, still held vast domains and a large number of subjects. While Brandenburg's population had decreased by half during the Thirty Years' War, Prussia was not hit as hard. Still, the situation Frederick William found himself in was not an enviable one.

At first, Frederick William relied on the guidance of his mother. She sought to clarify and quantify the problems facing the Hohenzollerns. It was determined that the continued war against the Swedes was too costly, but upsetting the alliance with the Habsburgs was equally impossible. No solutions were forthcoming.

However, Frederick William immediately realized the need for an effective, possibly permanent army. He did not dismiss Schwarzenberg but instead gradually diminished his powers to the point of insignificance. Frederick also tried to appease the nobles, whom he was supposed to consult on important matters, but he found them more concerned with their own gains than the needs of the nation. Their main complaint was against the army running amok.

Frederick agreed to reduce the army in Brandenburg, which was seemingly in contradiction to his desire for a standing army. Yet it was not a true contradiction. The army in Brandenburg was a motley crew of ill-trained troops who were a worse menace to the people than previous invading armies. Their combat value was dubious at best. For Frederick to build the army he wanted, he had to dissolve the current one.

In 1641, Schwarzenberg died unexpectedly. A few months later, an armistice with Sweden was concluded. Frederick William had to walk a fine line. While he could not continue the war with the Swedes, the ceasefire greatly concerned King Vladislav IV of Poland. Frederick William, as duke of Prussia, was a vassal to the Polish crown, so he kept Vladislav largely in the dark about his dealings with the Swedes.

In the same year as the peace deal with Sweden, Frederick William was able to reassert his power over Prussia and was granted the ability to impose an excise tax, which would become one of the most important sources of funds for Brandenburg-Prussia. The nobility of Prussia also benefited from this tax, so it helped to keep them satisfied and unlikely to cause trouble for the elector.

The social dynamics of Brandenburg-Prussia were particularly complicated since medieval serfdom was still practiced in areas like Pomerania and parts of the Uckermark. In both Prussia and Brandenburg, there were high and low nobility. In Prussia, east of the River Elbe, rural society was stratified. At the top were peasants who owned large farms and fulfilled their obligations by providing horses and laborers to their lord. Below them came cottagers with smaller plots of land (less than thirty hectares) who owed manual service. Then there were the cottagers who worked as full-time laborers during harvest season. At the bottom were servants who lived in or near the lord's premises and served him directly. These peasants could not leave the estate, get married, or learn a trade without their lord's permission. Serfs could be bought and sold like livestock.

To the west of the Elbe, the situation was not nearly as strict. In dealing with the nobility, Frederick William had to remember each noble's standing and culture. He also had to deal with different religious beliefs. While Frederick William was a Calvinist, most of his subjects were Lutheran. So, he adopted a stance of general religious tolerance.

In 1644, Frederick began to build his army, cautiously at first. He entrusted recruitment to his close confidant, Johann von Norprath. Norprath conducted the recruitment in the Lower Rhine region to avoid the suspicions of the Swedes. Garrisons in Brandenburg and Prussia were also increased. Frederick's goal was a well-trained standing army, and by 1646, he had about three thousand recruits in Cleves. The money to pay the soldiers came mostly from Prussia, but the payments were kept secret from both the Swedes and the nobles. The various sources of funds were kept so secret that many remain unknown to this day. Frederick William did raise some taxes without the consent of the nobles, which met with strong opposition.

Then, in 1648, what must have seemed like an endless war was finally concluded when the Holy Roman Empire signed a peace treaty with Sweden and then another with France. These treaties became known as the Peace of Westphalia and marked the end of the Thirty Years' War. It had been a war primarily centered around Holy Roman Emperor Ferdinand II's desire to see Roman Catholicism as the only religion in the Holy Roman Empire, but it had spread into a war that engulfed much of Europe and decimated Germany's population. It was one of the longest and most destructive wars in European history. Elector Frederick William had never experienced European peace until the treaties of Westphalia were signed.

Brandenburg-Prussia did not profit much from the Peace of Westphalia, except for the end, if temporary, of foreign armies marching across its borders. Frederick's nation remained relatively insignificant and was vulnerable partly because the east and west were separated, with the Swedes gaining the Pomeranian region after the war. Frederick's role as elector in the Holy Roman Empire did not afford him as much leverage, and his role as a vassal to the king of Poland was a burden. This was especially true in 1655 when war broke out between Poland and Sweden. Due to Poland's internal weaknesses, Frederick William abandoned his liege lord. The Swedes were victorious. They, in turn, imposed overlordship on Prussia.

The king of Poland, John Casimir, had been forced out of his kingdom but soon returned with greater support. Frederick William put his new army to the test in the three-day Battle of Warsaw. The army proved more than effective. When Austria and Russia threw their support behind Poland, Frederick William took the opportunity to demand that Sweden withdraw the bonds of vassalage and recognize Frederick as the sovereign duke of Prussia in his own right in exchange for his support of Sweden in the war. The Swedes agreed to those terms in the Treaty of Labiau in 1656.

The next year, Holy Roman Emperor Ferdinand III died. The imperial election would not occur until July 1658, when Ferdinand III's son, Leopold, came of age. Frederick William's electoral vote would be valuable in that election, but he had already secured his greatest prize months earlier. During the Second Northern War, Frederick William had switched sides from Sweden to Poland. Poland desperately needed his military support. In September 1657, in the Treaty of Wehlau, King John II Casimir of Poland agreed to end Prussia's vassalage. After more than a century as a Polish fief, Prussia was finally sovereign.

Sweden felt betrayed by Frederick William's actions and renewed hostilities with Brandenburg-Prussia. Frederick responded by securing an alliance with Austria and Poland. Frederick took a force of thirty thousand men composed of Brandenburg, imperial, and Polish troops.

They attacked the Swedes and drove them out of Schleswig and Holstein, just south of Denmark.

The victory was short-lived, as both the Holy Roman Empire and Poland gave up their support. In 1660, a peace was settled between Brandenburg-Prussia and Sweden in the Treaty of Oliva. All occupied territories were restored to their pre-war owners. Frederick had conquered most of Swedish Pomerania, but he was forced to give it back to the Swedes. His dream of uniting all of Pomerania under Brandenburg rule would have to wait.

After twenty years of rule, Frederick William's only successes appeared to be the formation of a standing army and the sovereignty of Prussia. These were certainly great successes, but Frederick William was an ambitious ruler who desired more. He mainly wanted to turn his nation into a formidable European power at all costs. The sovereignty of Prussia at least removed an avenue of power for the nobles, who often conspired with the Poles to undermine the rule of the elector. Frederick decided to pursue a policy of absolute authority, which the nobles quickly opposed.

The heart of the opposition was in Königsberg under the chairman of the city council, Hieronymus Roth. Frederick William left Danzig and landed with two thousand men. They marched into the city center. Faced with overwhelming force, the citizens gave Roth up. He was found guilty of treason and imprisoned for the rest of his life in the fortress of Peitz. A worse fate was met by Colonel Christian Ludwig von Kalckstein, who openly opposed the elector and managed to flee to Poland, only to be captured by Frederick William's men. He was beheaded in 1672. The message was clear. The nobles could no longer rely on Polish protection.

Frederick William soon instituted taxes and stationed troops in Königsberg without the approval of the nobles. He was met with no opposition. He faced even less opposition in establishing absolute authority in Brandenburg.

His next goal was a centralized and uniform government for all the lands he controlled. To do this, Frederick William introduced a uniform system of taxation. Despite the benefits, it was still not enough to pay for a peacetime army of seven thousand and a wartime army of almost thirty thousand troops. So, he relied on subsidies from larger allies like France, Spain, the Netherlands, Denmark, and Austria. These allies came and went with great frequency. And it was not just his allies that he could not fully trust. He also could not depend on the officers in his army. Frederick William tended to rely on foreign-born generals, the most well known being Field Marshal von Derfflinger, who was an Austrian of humble origins.

In the late 1660s and into the 1670s, Brandenburg-Prussia was caught in the machinations of the absolute monarch of France, Louis XIV. France was sometimes an ally and sometimes an enemy. Louis ran political circles around the likes of Frederick William. In December 1674, the elector received the alarming news that a Swedish army, allied with France, had invaded Brandenburg. Frederick William's army had already arrived at the winter quarters on the other side of central Germany. The challenge of getting the army to Brandenburg fell to Derfflinger, who divided his forces into smaller sections to increase mobility while keeping communication open.

In just two weeks, the army was back in Brandenburg. The Swedes, surprised by the sudden arrival and unaware of the Prussians' true numbers, quickly fell back. Derfflinger caught up to them. Though he had fewer troops and less artillery, the Swedes suffered a demoralizing defeat at the Battle of Fehrbellin. This feat helped to bolster the reputation of not just the Brandenburg-Prussian army but also of Frederick William himself, who was soon being hailed as the "Great Elector."

Derfflinger followed this success with a broader campaign in Swedish Pomerania. Frederick William realized he might finally be able to evict the Swedes if he continued the push. He allied himself with Denmark, whose fleet pressured Swedish positions in the Baltic. The campaign became protracted and lasted into 1677. Frederick William's goal was to capture the city of Stettin to secure control of the Oder River. After a siege and bombardment by land and sea, the city paid homage to him in January of 1678.

However, Frederick William's hopes for Brandenburg-Prussia to be respected by the great powers of the day were short-lived. France encouraged Sweden to undertake another campaign against Brandenburg in the winter of 1678/79. As his allies dwindled, Frederick concluded the Peace of Saint-Germain-en-Laye in June of 1679, which returned Pomerania to Sweden.

Perhaps recognizing the futility of opposing France, Frederick William instead decided to join Louis XIV. Secret negotiations began. Frederick hoped to turn the alliance against the hated Swedes, while Louis hoped for Prussian assistance in the annexation of German territories, which Louis chose to call "reunions."

In 1681, when Louis's army besieged and captured the imperial city of Strasbourg, Frederick William's alliance with the French made him a traitor in the eyes of many. However, Frederick kept his alliance with Louis, and in 1683, it seemed to bear fruit when the French agreed to drive Sweden out of Germany. Yet, these treaties were never ratified, and Frederick William's dreams of obtaining Pomerania would never be realized.

In that same year, France found the Holy Roman Empire completely distracted by the presence of an Ottoman army outside the city of Vienna. The Battle of Vienna, which was waged between the Holy Roman Empire and the Polish-Lithuanian Commonwealth and the Ottoman Empire and its vassals, was a decisive victory for the Holy Roman Empire and Poland. It was the turning point in the expansion of the Ottomans into Europe. They would gain no more territory after the battle, and many of the lands they had conquered in Hungary would be returned to Emperor Leopold I. Brandenburg-Prussia was not involved in the fight at all, and its absence was duly noted.

France abandoned Frederick William as an ally, so Frederick tried to ally himself with the Habsburgs and the Holy Roman Empire, but he was rebuffed. He was told that as an elector, he had a duty to support the empire. Peace was finally settled between France and the Holy Roman Empire, which was much to the benefit of France. There was no profit for Frederick or even the Germans.

As Frederick William approached the end of his life, his legacy seemed uncertain at best. In 1682, he gave a charter to the Brandenburg Africa Company in the hopes of getting in on the profitable slave trade. This company founded two colonies, Gross-Friedrichsburg and Fort Dorothea. Neither colony was profitable during Frederick's lifetime.

While Brandenburg-Prussia had become a formidable power, it was not the great power that Frederick had hoped for. It was often a pawn in political affairs and subject to the whims of France, the Holy Roman Empire, and Sweden. It was not a great commercial power either. Yet Frederick William is still remembered as the "Great Elector," not because he raised Prussia to the heights of a great European power, but because he laid the foundation upon which later leaders built Prussia's power.

After a reign of forty-eight years, Frederick William died at the age of sixty-eight. He left behind a military and government organization that had been much improved since he had taken over at twenty years old. It was a system that would greatly benefit the leaders who followed him.

Chapter 5: Prussia's Age of Enlightenment

King Frederick II's Roundtable at Sanssouci by Adolph von Menzel features Frederick II, King of Prussia, as well as Enlightenment thinkers Voltaire, d'Argens, La Mettrie, and Algarotti, among others.‘

The Great Elector left behind an army of thirty thousand troops when he died. The question of how to pay for this army led his successors to continue attracting immigrants to Prussia. The revocation of the Edict of Nantes in 1685 had brought some twenty thousand French and Walloon Huguenots into his domain. These emigrants possessed highly developed commercial and industrial skills and were often better educated than the native population.

Besides the army and these industrious new citizens, Frederick William's greatest legacy was the sovereignty of Prussia, which he had secured in 1657. The Great Elector's successor, his son Frederick III, had a singular goal. While he left the administration of his nation to a series of prime ministers, Frederick sought to raise his title of duke of Prussia to the title of king. His situation as the elector of Brandenburg made him technically a vassal of the Holy Roman Empire, which meant that he could not be a king there. However, as the sovereign ruler of Prussia, he felt he had a right to a royal title.

Yet, while Holy Roman Emperor Leopold I did not need to confer the crown on Frederick, the emperor did need to give his approval and recognition. This meant that Brandenburg-Prussia would need to maintain its alliance with the Holy Roman Empire at all costs. Negotiations began just two years after Frederick William's death. Leopold agreed to the deal in the Crown Treaty of November 1700 after a war with France erupted. Leopold needed Prussian troops. In January 1701, Frederick crowned himself King Frederick I, King in Prussia. He chose "in Prussia" instead of "of Prussia" because West Prussia was still part of Poland, and he wanted to avoid objections from the Polish monarchy, which viewed the coronation as illegal.

King Frederick I's reign was also noted for the founding of the Prussian Academy of Arts in 1696 and the Academy of Sciences in 1700. He died in 1713 and was followed by his son, King Frederick William I, known as the "Soldier King."

Pragmatic and harsh, Frederick William cut many of his father's expenditures, including shutting down the Academy of Sciences as an economic measure. He concerned himself with every detail of the ruling of his country and is considered an absolutist monarch. Unwilling to spend the money needed to maintain them, Frederick William sold off the West African colony his father established and disbanded the Prussian Navy. He made considerable changes to military training and equipment. He died at the age of fifty-one in 1740, leaving the country to his son, King Frederick II, also known as "the Great."

What followed was a flowering of arts and sciences that made Prussia a center for the European Enlightenment. Frederick II reopened the Academy of Sciences in 1740, inviting thinkers of all kinds to come to Prussia to study and teach.

Let's now take a look at some of the leading Enlightenment luminaries with ties to the Prussian state.

Christian Wolff.[5]

Christian Wolff (1679–1754)

Christian Wolff was born on January 24th, 1679, in Breslau in Silesia (part of modern-day Poland) to parents of modest means. He was able to attend school and eventually went to the University of Jena to study theology, physics, and mathematics. He then moved to the University of Leipzig in 1702, where his work caught the attention of many academics, including the German philosopher Gottfried Wilhelm Leibniz. The two struck up a correspondence that lasted until Leibniz died in 1716. Wolff took up a position as a professor of mathematics at the University of Halle in Prussia. There, he lectured in math and natural science, eventually tackling traditional philosophy as well.

He published a series of textbooks on logic, metaphysics, ethics, politics, and physics from 1713 to 1723. These textbooks became popular partly because the first editions were written in the German vernacular; Latin versions were printed later. This allowed greater access to Wolff's concepts among his countrymen.

He enjoyed a stellar reputation among other intellectuals but ran afoul of the theology department at Halle (a group of Pietist Lutherans) when he espoused the doctrine of predeterminism. The escalating conflict with the Pietists, including controversy over his lectures on Chinese philosophy and their implications for the autonomy of moral reasoning, led to the involvement of King Frederick William I. He banished the philosopher from Prussia in 1723, only giving him forty-eight hours to leave or face execution.

Wolff's expulsion only enhanced his reputation and brought him to the attention of other Enlightenment luminaries like Voltaire. He accepted a position at the University of Marburg. In 1733, attempts were made to entice Wolff back to Prussia (in 1734, Prussia rescinded the 1723 arrest warrant and offered him various positions), but Wolff declined these overtures. However, with the ascension of King Frederick II in 1740, the enlightened monarch made Wolff an offer he could not refuse. Wolff accepted the king's invitation to return to Halle, initially as vice-chancellor and later as chancellor of the university in 1743. Christian Wolff died in Halle in 1754.

Wolff is often seen as the intellectual bridge between Leibniz and Immanuel Kant and is often described as a follower of Leibniz. This characterization is misleading for several reasons. While Leibniz was older than Wolff, the majority of Leibniz's most important philosophical works, including *The Principles of Nature and Grace*, *Monadology*, and *New Essays on Human Understanding*, were published posthumously, after Wolff had already developed and published his own philosophical system. The correspondence between the two thinkers primarily was over mathematics, which was Wolff's focus at the time. Leibniz himself even commented that Wolff knew very little of his philosophical ideas, writing, "Mr. Wolff has adopted some of my opinions, but since he is very busy with teaching, especially in mathematics, and we have not had much correspondence together on philosophy, he can know very little about my opinions beyond those which I have published." Because of this, it is important to see Wolff as a great independent thinker of the Enlightenment, especially for his work in bringing new philosophical thought to Prussia.

Pierre Louis Maupertuis.[6]

Pierre Louis Maupertuis (1698–1759)

Born in Saint-Malo, France, in 1698 to a moderately wealthy family of merchants, Maupertuis was privately tutored in mathematics. He eventually moved to Paris to establish himself as a mathematician. In 1723, he was admitted into the Académie des Sciences. He developed and extended the work of Isaac Newton, whose theories were less widely accepted on the Continent outside England. In 1736, he led the French Geodesic Mission sent by King Louis XV to Lapland. This expedition helped prove a theory held by Newtonians that the Earth was oblate and not prolate by measuring the length of a degree of arc of the meridian. This garnered Maupertuis a good deal of respect and acclaim within European scientific circles.

Four years after the expedition, he was invited to Berlin by King Frederick II. After being taken prisoner at the Battle of Mollwitz in 1741 and released, he returned to Paris, where he was elected director of the Académie des Sciences in 1742. He returned to Brandenburg-Prussia in 1745, and Frederick chose him to be the president of the Royal Prussian Academy of Sciences in 1746. This organization was founded by Frederick I in 1700 upon the advice of German philosopher Gottfried Wilhelm Leibniz. It was a French-language institution because, at the time, French was the language of science and culture.

Maupertuis served as president of the Royal Academy until 1753, when the controversy with Voltaire and his deteriorating health caused him to leave Berlin, effectively ending his presidency. Though he briefly returned in 1754, he left again for France and spent his final years traveling for his health, dying in Basel in 1759. He was often at odds with fellow philosophers and had well-known controversies with Johann Samuel König and Voltaire.

Voltaire.[7]

Voltaire (1694–1778)

Frederick the Great and Voltaire began a correspondence in 1736 when Frederick was still the crown prince. Frederick was raised in Prussia but became deeply influenced by French Enlightenment culture. They shared a firm conviction in the importance of religious tolerance backed by skepticism in traditional religions. Frederick saw in Voltaire another luminary to add to his growing collection in Berlin. Voltaire saw in Frederick a great philosopher king, an enlightened monarch who would finally create a free, just, and peaceful nation. They would both be disappointed.

In 1750, Voltaire came to Brandenburg-Prussia after numerous invitations from King Frederick II. He was welcomed by the other French expatriates there, including Maupertuis. He was given the position of chamberlain, which had very few duties, and was given an annual salary of twenty thousand French livres. He had rooms at the Sanssouci and Charlottenburg palaces.

After approximately two and a half years, Voltaire angered Frederick, first by his involvement in a financial scandal and then after the publication of his satirical book *Docteur Akakia,* in which he criticized Maupertuis's theories and questioned the mathematician's ethics. Frederick ordered official copies of *Docteur Akakia* to be confiscated and publicly burned. Voltaire offered to resign his position. Frederick initially refused but then accepted.

However, as Voltaire was heading back to France, he was detained in Frankfurt by Frederick's agents for over three weeks. This detention was over manuscripts of poetry Frederick had loaned to Voltaire and wanted back. It was a prime example to Voltaire that Frederick was not the enlightened monarch he had hoped for. He was just another despot ruling according to his whim. Voltaire would satirize Frederick in many works. In his posthumous publication, *Mémoires pour Servir à la Vie de M. de Voltaire,* he explicitly mentioned Frederick's homosexuality, describing how the king regularly invited pages, young cadets, and lieutenants from his regiment to have coffee with him and then withdrew with the favorite, framing this in a manner intended to degrade the king.

Their eventual clash seems, in hindsight, inevitable. While Frederick was a philosopher and king, he also tended toward authoritarian rule. Voltaire, ever the skeptic and challenger of the status quo, the epitome of the Enlightenment rebel, could never have survived long under

Frederick's thumb. Despite their falling out, they continued to correspond. After the Seven Years' War, they largely reconciled, though they would never again meet in person.

Carl Philipp Emanuel Bach.[8]

Carl Philipp Emanuel Bach (1714–1788)

C. P. E. Bach was the fifth child and second surviving son of Johann Sebastian Bach and his first wife, Maria Barbara. The younger Bach attended university at Leipzig and then at Frankfurt-on-the-Oder in 1735. He studied law but was trained in music by his father. In 1738, he obtained an appointment in Berlin, serving Crown Prince Frederick of Prussia. When the prince ascended the throne as King Frederick II (the Great) in 1740, Bach joined the royal orchestra. He was renowned for playing the clavier, a keyboard instrument, and composed over one hundred sonatas and concert pieces for the harpsichord and clavichord.

Bach spent much of his time in Berlin, which, under the direction of Frederick the Great, had become a center for arts and culture. Bach became friends with other musicians and literary figures like Gotthold Ephraim Lessing. In 1746, he rose to the post of chamber musician and wrote several well-regarded pieces, including symphonies, cantatas, and other sacred vocal works. In 1753, he published his influential treatise on the playing of keyboard instruments, which was highly valued by Haydn and Beethoven.

In 1768, Bach was allowed to leave his post in Brandenburg-Prussia to become the director of music in Hamburg. There, he focused on choral work, which gained widespread appreciation. He died in Hamburg in 1788.

Jean-Baptiste de Boyer.⁹

Jean-Baptiste de Boyer, Marquis d'Argens (1704–1771)

Born into a devout Catholic family, Jean-Baptiste de Boyer, Marquis d'Argens, was a rationalist author and critic of the Catholic Church. He was disinherited by his family and began a career as a writer, publishing a book in 1735 and the six-volume *Lettres juives* between 1736 and 1740. In 1742, he accepted an invitation from Frederick the Great to be the royal chamberlain in Berlin. He remained there for most of his career.

He met and befriended Voltaire, but unlike Voltaire, d'Argens was not just opposed to absolute monarchy. He was also highly critical of religious authority and traditional institutions. Interestingly, he does not appear to have quarreled with Frederick the Great like his more famous friend. D'Argens finally returned to France in 1769.

Julien Offray de la Mettrie.[10]

Julien Offray de la Mettrie (1709–1751)

Mettrie, like his fellow countryman Maupertuis, was born in Saint-Malo to a prosperous merchant family. He attended the Collège du Plessis in Paris and was initially interested in becoming a clergyman, although he later turned away from the church. Mettrie attended the Collège d'Harcourt, where he studied natural philosophy before graduating in 1728. He then studied under the renowned Dutch physician Hermann Boerhaave.

Mettrie returned to his home region of Saint-Malo to begin practicing as a physician. He went on to be appointed surgeon in the French Guards during the War of the Austrian Succession. It was around this time that he made the acquaintance of Maupertuis.

While in Paris, Mettrie suffered from a fever, which led him to believe that mental faculties like emotion were accounted for by organic changes in the brain and nervous system. The publication of his *Histoire naturelle de l'âme* caused an outcry, and he was forced to take refuge in Holland. There, he wrote his most famous work, *L'Homme machine* (*Man a Machine*), which espoused materialistic and partly atheistic concepts.

In 1748, Mettrie was forced to leave Holland for Berlin due to hostility against his works. In Berlin, he joined Maupertuis. Frederick the Great named him the court reader and allowed him to practice as a physician. Mettrie wrote *Discours sur le bonheur*, which appalled many Enlightenment thinkers with its purely hedonistic and sensualistic rhetoric. For this, Mettrie was largely written out of the history of the Enlightenment for about one hundred years.

He died in Berlin at a feast at which he was said to have devoured a large amount of food and died of a gastronomic illness as a result. Frederick the Great delivered his eulogy, in which he described Mettrie as a good devil and fine physician but a terrible writer.

Francesco Algarotti.[11]

Francesco Algarotti (1712–1764)

It is believed that Francesco Algarotti, a Venetian polymath, became Frederick the Great's close companion when the Italian was touring northern Europe with Lord Baltimore in 1739. Frederick came to the throne the next year and began to correspond with Algarotti, who had not only an encyclopedic mind and a handsome face but was also known to have had amorous relationships with both men and women. Frederick referred to Algarotti as his "dear swan of Padua."

It was through Algarotti that Frederick obtained some of his most prized works of art. One statue, reportedly of a nude Roman boy, was said to have been placed just in front of the king's bedroom window at Sanssouci, the king's new summer palace. Frederick made Algarotti a count, as well as Algarotti's brother. Together, they toured Prussia and met with Voltaire. However, it must be noted that Algarotti—and perhaps Frederick as well—were not interested in a monogamous relationship. Algarotti is thought to have carried on various romantic liaisons across Europe.

Algarotti's greatest contribution to the Enlightenment was perhaps his desire to spread the teachings of Isaac Newton throughout the Continent. He was a noted art collector and acquired several important works of the 18th century. He died of tuberculosis while living in Pisa.

Immanuel Kant.[19]

Immanuel Kant (1724–1804)

Immanuel Kant, perhaps the last great Enlightenment thinker, was born in Königsberg, the capital of East Prussia. Unlike the many French, German, and Italian philosophers, artists, and musicians who were drawn to Prussia by the magnetism of Frederick the Great, Kant was truly a native son.

Kant's father was a harness maker of modest means. Like the theologians of the University of Halle, Kant's parents were Pietists, an evangelical branch of Lutheranism. Kant went to a Pietist school as a child, where the focus was on classical learning, religious instruction, and moral discipline. It could be said that Kant's forced focus on emotion and dependence on divine grace helped form his later interest in autonomy and rationality. While Kant might have hated his schooling, he loved his parents, who taught him hard work, honesty, and independence.

He attended the University of Königsberg, then known as the Albertina. He quickly found a passion for philosophy, which incorporated mathematics, physics, logic, ethics, metaphysics, and natural law. There, he was introduced to the work of Christian Wolff and Leibniz. Still, there were many in the faculty of the school who opposed Wolff's views. Kant's favorite professor, Martin Knutzen, was a Pietist influenced by the English philosopher John Locke. Through Knutzen, Kant was introduced to the works of Isaac Newton.

After university, Kant acted as a private tutor to children in East Prussia. In 1755, after both of his parents had died and his finances remained insecure, he returned to the Albertina as a lecturer. He would teach philosophy there for the next forty years.

In 1755, Kant published several works, one of which was *Universal Natural History and Theory of the Heavens*, in which he developed what would become known as the nebular hypothesis on the formation of the solar system. However, the book was published anonymously and initially had little impact. In the years after this seeming failure, Kant gained a reputation as an excellent lecturer and an intellectual. His finances were bolstered by the large number of students who attended his classes; they paid him directly.

Kant unleashed another round of publications in the early 1760s. These works of philosophy helped give him a wider audience, but they were not seen as particularly groundbreaking. They drew on British philosophers like David Hume, Francis Hutcheson, Newton, and the Swiss thinker Rousseau. In 1770, Kant gained the position he had longed for: the chair of philosophy and logic at the Albertina. With this, he became more financially secure and expanded his lecture repertoire.

Kant published a new work known as the *Inaugural Dissertation,* which marked a significant departure from both German rationalism and British sentimentalism. Kant introduced concepts that he would keep for the rest of his life. For instance, he believed understanding consists of both sensibility and reason, that time and space are forms relative to human sensibility, and that moral judgments are based purely on reason. Kant worked for a decade refining his ideas and then, in 1781, released another burst of publications, including *Critique of Pure Reason* (second edition in 1787), *Metaphysical Foundations of Natural Science* (1786), and *Critique of Practical Reason* (1788).

With these and many other publications, Kant came to dominate German philosophy. He gained widespread acclaim and international fame. Kant continued to publish into the 1790s and was once even censured by the new king of Prussia, Frederick William II, nephew of Frederick the Great. Many German philosophers began to move away from Kantian ideas in order to distinguish themselves in the competitive academic environment of German universities.

Kant retired from teaching in 1796. He died in 1804 at the age of seventy-nine, leaving behind a library's worth of work for future generations to ponder.

Chapter 6: Frederick the Great

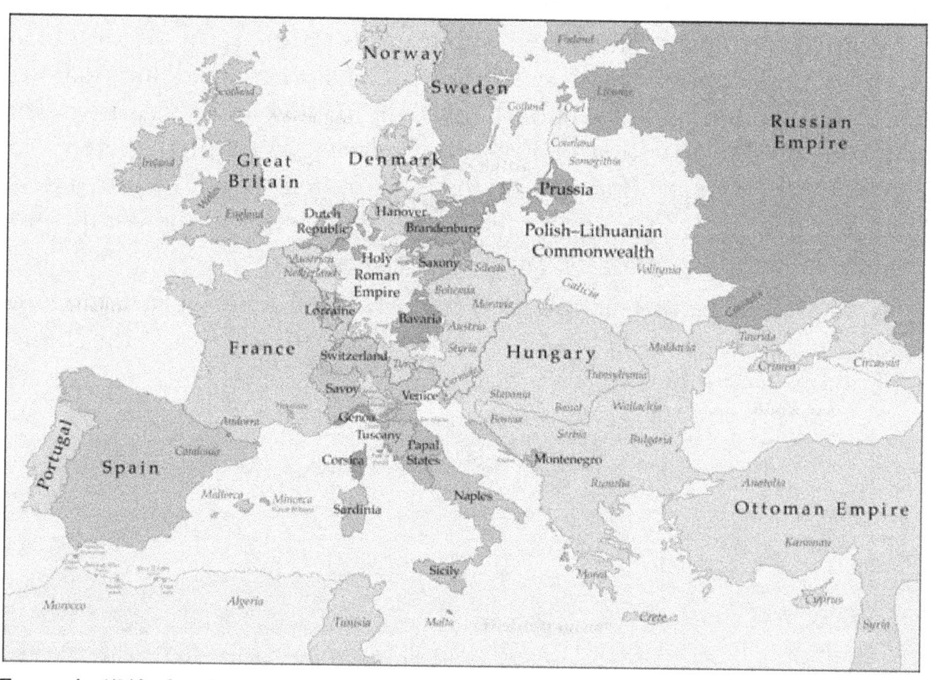

Europe in 1740 when Frederick the Great came to the throne. Notice Brandeburg and Prussia.[13]

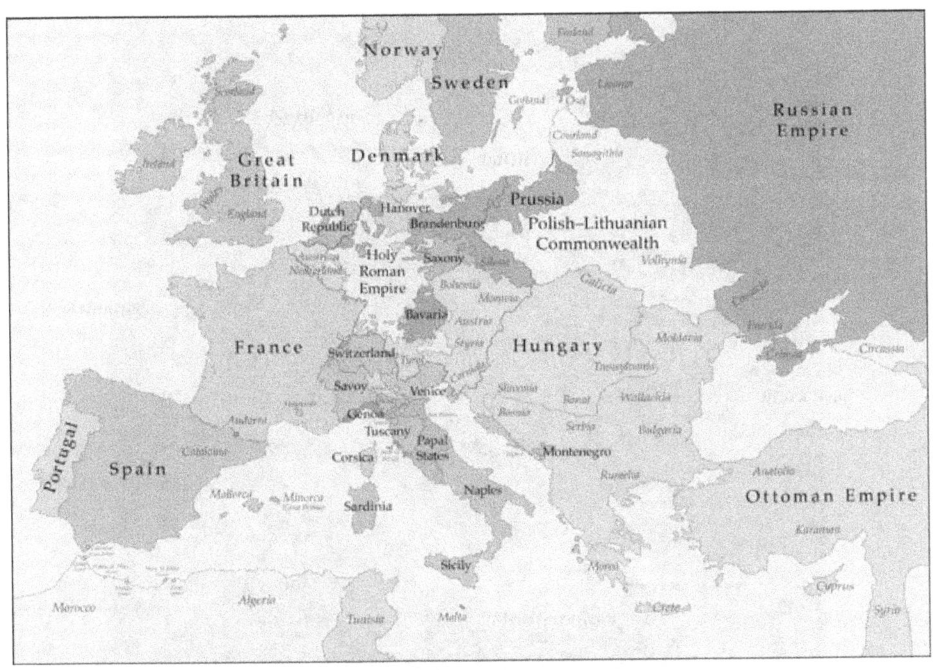

Europe at the time of Frederick's death.[14]

The crown prince of Prussia's relationship with his father was problematic. King Frederick William thought young Fritz, as he was then called, was too enamored with French culture, which he saw as effeminate and overindulgent. The king hated everything French and flew into a rage at the mere mention of the great European power. Fritz grew to hate his father's strict rule.

A crucial moment in the prince's life was when he planned with some compatriots to leave Prussia for England but was caught before he could make his escape. The king brought Fritz up on charges of desertion and had him court-martialed. The prince was saved when the court rejected the charge, but his companion and possible lover, Lieutenant von Katte, was sentenced to death and beheaded in front of Fritz. The king toyed with taking Fritz out of the succession but was eventually convinced against it. How much the episode affected Fritz remains unclear, but afterward, he appeared to mature and began earnestly preparing himself for the throne.

Crown Prince Frederick, known as "Fritz."[15]

Fritz drifted away from his Calvinist upbringing. Unlike his father, he came to believe that royal power came from the state, not from God. Frederick, as a religious skeptic, created a devotion to duty and the state. By then, he was twenty-eight years old and prepared for what would come.

In May of 1740, King Frederick William, the "Soldier King," died in Potsdam. His son, King Frederick II, took the crown. With it came a large and disciplined standing army. Prussia was a highly militarized state. The Prussian infantry was arguably unrivaled in discipline and firepower. His title, like his grandfather and father before him, was still "King in Prussia." Frederick II recognized that Brandenburg-Prussia would always be at a disadvantage as long as its territory remained fragmented. One of his goals was to acquire territory to connect and round off his kingdom.

Frederick's loyalty to the state did not falter once he acquired the crown. Many times, he gave instructions that if he were ever captured, then his counselors should do nothing to save him. "I am king only when I am free," he told them. "I shall sacrifice myself for the state ... no ransom must be offered."

The monarch subordinated himself to the state, but this must not be confused with the people, for they, too, served the state and had to be willing to sacrifice themselves for the needs of the kingdom. Frederick would be every bit the absolutist monarch as his father and the king he most admired, Louis XIV. Still, he held to his Enlightenment ideals. He limited the use of torture, reorganized the Academy of Sciences with Maupertuis at its head, and began construction of the Berlin State Opera. He also remained focused on his goal of turning Prussia into a great power. He did not have to wait long to make his move.

In October 1740, Holy Roman Emperor Charles VI died unexpectedly, leaving the Habsburg lands to his daughter Maria Theresa of Austria. Russia was preoccupied with the death of the tsarina, who died just three days before. Frederick felt confident in challenging Maria Theresa's right to the lands and asserted his own right to the richest of the Austrian provinces, Silesia.

His claims were ambiguous. He claimed it through some old treaties with the House of Hohenzollern, but it was still enough of a pretense for Frederick to prepare for war. He approached his ministers and generals to determine the best way to capture Silesia. One minister suggested diplomacy. Frederick instead decided to march into Silesia. What followed would be known as the First Silesian War.

Frederick was hedging his bets on quick and decisive action. The occupation of Silesia was relatively easy until Frederick was surprised by the arrival of an Austrian army in the Battle of Mollwitz. While the Prussian cavalry fell into disarray and Frederick actually took flight for fear of being captured, the Prussian infantry persevered and won the day. Frederick took the opportunity to fine-tune the cavalry. The French and the Electorate of Bavaria joined the War of the Austrian Succession against the Austrians, with Great Britain and Russia joining the Austrian side. Charles of Bavaria was soon elected Holy Roman Emperor Charles VII.

In the Battle of Chotusitz, Frederick's new cavalry performed much better, but it was the infantry again that won the field. It was a major victory for Frederick and resulted in the Treaty of Breslau in 1742, in which Prussia gained all of Silesia and Glatz County. The Austrians only retained a small area called Austrian (or Czech) Silesia.

However, the peace did not last long. After Maria Theresa's Austrian forces expelled the French beyond the Rhine, Frederick drove his army toward Austria, beginning the Second Silesian War in 1744.

At first, Frederick's advance into Austrian territory was unsuccessful. He had no support from his ally, France, while Austria received troops from Saxony and had the assistance of the British. He lost almost seventeen thousand men to desertion in a few months' time. In January of 1745, Holy Roman Emperor Charles VII died, and Bavaria made peace with Austria. Frederick decided, against the military theory of the time, to withdraw to Silesia and wait for his enemy to come to him.

An Austrian and Saxon army of seventy thousand soon crossed the Sudeten Mountains to Hohenfriedberg. Contrary to Austrian expectations, Frederick attacked their left flank, pushing through the Saxons and then the Austrians. Their total casualties numbered around ten thousand. It was a dramatic Prussian victory and restored Frederick's reputation. Still, the Austrians did not surrender.

Maria Theresa's husband was crowned Holy Roman Emperor Francis I, despite Frederick's vote against him. In the fall of 1745, Frederick was preparing to winter in Silesia when he received word that the Austrians planned to attack. He had just twenty-two thousand troops; the Austrian commander, Prince Charles of Lorraine, led an army of thirty-nine thousand. Frederick decided to strike first.

This time, it was the Prussian cavalry that distinguished itself. Frederick gained another impressive victory. His reputation soared, and the prefix "the Great" began to enter the public consciousness. The Prussian Army pushed on and defeated the Saxons in December. Maria Theresa finally ended her campaign to recapture Silesia, and peace was concluded on Christmas Day 1745.

Frederick proceeded to open Silesia's resources to the rest of Prussia. While he still held the formal title "King in Prussia," by this point, many referred to him simply as "King of Prussia." Frederick focused on domestic affairs, furthering judicial reforms and establishing universal policies throughout his nation.

The ten-year period after the Second Silesian War was the time of the informal "Round Table of Sanssouci," where Frederick entertained Enlightenment thinkers at his new summer palace. Frederick composed flute music, which he performed, showcasing a genuine talent for musical composition beyond that of a mere amateur. In the early 1750s, Frederick finally met Voltaire, and a relationship based on admiration and hope quickly turned to one of criticism and disappointment on both sides.

All the while, Frederick continued to build his army and enrich his war chest. At the same time, it seemed his enemies were encircling him. In the early 1750s, Austria and Russia began aligning diplomatically. By 1756, they had a formal alliance aimed mainly at countering Prussian power. In 1755, Great Britain concluded the Convention of Westminster with Frederick, which promised mutual neutrality and protection for Hanover during the imminent Anglo-French war over the North American colonies. Frederick had hoped for an agreement with France as well, but France instead entered into a defensive alliance with Austria as part of the Diplomatic Revolution (the reversal of long-standing alliances in Europe). The Franco-Prussian relationship dissolved in 1756, and the French showed no interest in renewal.

In the ring forming around Prussia, Frederick felt Russia was the greatest military threat, but he believed Russia would only attack if goaded by the Austrians. Frederick was right to fear the Russian military, but he underestimated their own interest in curbing Prussian power. In 1756, Russian leadership began planning a military campaign to counter Prussia's growing influence in central Europe.

Throughout 1756, Russian and Austrian troop movements heightened Frederick's concern of an impending attack. Deciding on a preemptive strike, in August, he occupied Saxony. After a prolonged siege, the Saxon army capitulated in October and was forcibly incorporated into the Prussian Army. This would prove to be a mistake because entire units of Saxons soon deserted en masse. This began Prussia's involvement in the global war of the European great powers: the Seven Years' War (1756–1763).

France was suffering at the hands of the British and so turned its defensive alliance with Austria into an offensive one in 1757. Sweden also joined the anti-Prussian alliance, as did the Holy Roman Empire. Frederick moved his armies in the spring of 1757, which led to the Battle of Prague, in which the war hero Field Marshal Kurt von Schwerin was killed. Still, the Austrians suffered heavy losses, with casualties numbering around fifteen thousand, making it one of the bloodiest battles of the war.

This did not annihilate the Austrian army, which withdrew to the fortress of Prague. Frederick began to lay siege to the city. Another Austrian force was on the way to bring relief to those inside Prague. When Frederick faced this larger force at the Battle of Kolín, he was defeated. Soon after, the French and their allies advanced into Saxony. On November 5th, 1757, Frederick led an army of about twenty-two thousand men against a combined French and Imperial force of over forty thousand. The Prussians were able to surprise the enemy and completely rout their foe. Napoleon Bonaparte would later call Frederick's tactics in this battle, the Battle of Rossbach, the work of a genius. The French would no longer play a major role in the Seven Years' War in central Europe.

Idealized Frederick the Great as a standard bearer.[16]

Frederick had no time to celebrate. He soon learned that the Russians were attacking East Prussia and that the Austrians had invaded Silesia. He decided to attack the Austrians first, though they occupied the high ground and were entrenched. Frederick concentrated his forces at the Austrian center but at the last minute reformed and hit the unsuspecting left wing. The Battle of Leuthen was a resounding defeat for the Austrians, who fled to Bohemia.

The Russians, upon rumors of the death of Tsarina Elizabeth, withdrew from East Prussia in late 1757. The rumors turned out to be false. In 1758, the Russians returned and occupied Königsberg. Frederick responded, and the Prussians and Russians faced each other for the first time in open battle.

The Battle of Zorndorf lasted all day, with both sides displaying extreme tenacity and bravery. Only the coming of night ended the hostilities. At dawn, the Prussians were surprised to see the Russians had withdrawn from the field. The Russians suffered around sixteen thousand to seventeen thousand casualties, while Frederick lost about twelve thousand. It was not the resounding victory that Frederick had hoped for. Yet, the Prussians had stopped the Russians from driving further into Prussia and from linking up with Austrian forces.

Lack of material and men forced Frederick to fight a defensive war to secure his possessions, including Saxony. When a force of Russians and Austrians, about sixty thousand strong, pushed into his territory, Frederick met them at Kunersdorf in 1759. The Prussians were soundly defeated, and the king came close to being captured. The Russians and Austrians did not follow up on their success but went their separate ways to pursue their separate aims.

Frederick temporarily lost Dresden and had to abandon Saxony. The Austrians, with a force of around fifty thousand, planned to annihilate Frederick's army of roughly equal size. However, Frederick outmaneuvered his foe and won the Battle of Torgau in November of 1760. Still, he could not complete his objective of recapturing Dresden due to a continued lack of supplies and manpower. He raised troops from pressed foreigners and cadets as young as fourteen. He eventually gathered almost 100,000 troops, but their offensive capacity was doubtful.

Prussia's future looked grim, and it might have been if not for the timely death of Tsarina Elizabeth. She was succeeded to the throne by

Peter III, who was a great admirer of Frederick's. He reversed Russia's policy on Prussia and recommended peace. Peace was signed between Russia and Prussia in May 1762. Frederick had hopes of an alliance with Peter against the Austrians, but his dream ended with the overthrow and death of Peter III in July 1762.

However, France and Great Britain had agreed on peace, and soon, Maria Theresa finally agreed to end the conflict with Prussia. Frederick was forced to give up what he claimed in Saxony, but he retained Silesia. Frederick agreed to the treaty because he had, like much of Europe, tired of war for the time being. The Seven Years' War had been a huge drain on men and money. Nations had found themselves simply incapable of going on.

A period of reconstruction began. Frederick wanted to use the peace to build up his army. He had learned from his predecessors and from his own experience that a standing army was crucial to Prussia's survival and growth. Petty criminals and vagabonds were pressed into service. By 1776, the Prussian Army would number over 187,000 soldiers.

In 1764, a general crisis in trade and commerce struck Berlin, as well as Amsterdam and Hamburg. Frederick envisioned a novel approach to addressing such issues. He came up with a plan in which capital and money were concentrated in the hands of the state as well as manufacturing and trade. To this end, he proposed creating a central bank, the Preußische Giro- und Lehnbank. But the idea got no further because of pushback from merchants and the overwhelming issues of administration.

Frederick purchased a porcelain factory in Berlin, which became the Königliche Porzellan-Manufaktur, which still exists today as KPM Berlin. Under Frederick, the KPM became a model employer with regular working hours, no child labor, and health insurance coverage. Frederick was also the company's first great customer, ordering 200,000 Reichsthalers' worth of ceramics from the company's founding until his death.

Frederick forced the expansion of potato planting and large-scale dairy farming. The number of cattle in Prussian territory doubled by the end of the 18th century. He increased the excise tax on brandy, beer, and meat but abolished it on flour. The result was a significant increase in revenue—possibly up to 23.5 million thalers from 1766 to 1786. Much was spent on welfare purposes, but plenty was put back into the state treasury. The king attracted outside settlers. In the years after the Seven Years' War, the population increased by about 1.25 percent per year.

In 1764, Frederick the Great secured a formal alliance with Russia, strengthening ties between the two powers. Following the death of King Augustus III of Poland, a contested royal succession unfolded within the Polish-Lithuanian Commonwealth. With support from both Prussia and Russia, Stanisław August Poniatowski, a pro-Russian candidate, was elected king. The Russo-Prussian alliance allowed both states to exert influence over Polish affairs. In the years that followed, as Russia became embroiled in war with the Ottoman Empire (beginning in 1768) and internal unrest deepened in Poland, Frederick skillfully maneuvered politics. These developments culminated in the First Partition of Poland in 1772, in which Prussia, Russia, and Austria each annexed portions of Polish territory. The result was Prussian control of West Prussia, finally linking Prussia with Brandenburg.

In 1780, Frederick's great antagonist, Maria Theresa, died. Her son, Joseph II, succeeded her. Joseph tried to expand territorially, but Frederick checked him at every move. France, Britain, and Russia were too concerned with their own affairs to get involved in a central European squabble. Then, on August 17th, 1786, Frederick the Great died at the age of seventy-four. No other Prussian monarch had accomplished as much as he had.

Frederick's reign had not just brought Prussia onto the global stage, but he had also inspired future generations of Germans. As Goethe wrote of Frederick, "What mattered Prussia to us? It was the personality of the Great King which affected the emotions of us all." People, especially writers looking to define what it was to be German, looked to Frederick as the leader, regardless of whether they were Prussians and despite the fact that Frederick was typically critical of German writing, preferring the French in almost all art forms.

Frederick the Great's legacy is ambiguous to the modern reader. His idolization as the ultimate German "hero" and a paragon of duty and militarism has been stained by his later incorporation into Nazi propaganda. Adolf Hitler was a great fan of Frederick's and carried a portrait of the Prussian monarch with him, even in his bunker during the final days of World War II. After World War II, Frederick's role in history was downplayed, but renewed interest in him has emerged at the end of the 20th and into the 21st centuries.

Frederick's patronage of the arts is seen as a positive. His sense of duty to his country marks him as a clear example of Enlightenment absolutism, though his military efforts often contradict certain Enlightenment ideologies. Military historians regard him as a great leader and strategist, and his battles are still studied around the world. Napoleon was an admirer of the king. Frederick is still considered a model of "servant leadership," a concept in which the role of the leader is to serve the greater good.

Frederick also wrote several works in his lifetime. As crown prince, he received some notoriety for penning *Anti-Machiavel*, which attempted to argue against Machiavelli's principles in his Renaissance work *The Prince.* Several volumes by Frederick were published after his death, including a two-volume history of the Seven Years' War. Also published posthumously were two memoirs, *The History of My Own Times*, and an instruction book originally written to his generals. He is also remembered for his flute compositions.

Before Frederick became king, he was married to Elisabeth Christine of Brunswick-Wolfenbüttel-Bevern, who would be queen through his entire reign and would outlive him by eleven years. It is fairly certain that Frederick was gay and that this remained his primary orientation for most of his life. However, the exact nature of his relationships remains speculative. Frederick and Elisabeth's marriage remained childless, and Frederick would be succeeded by his nephew, Frederick William II. Certain letters survive that indicate quite clearly that Frederick had same-sex affairs with men, such as his secretary, Claude Darget. Voltaire commented openly about Frederick's homosexuality. Frederick's younger brother, Prince Henry, is also believed to have been gay.

Chapter 7: Prussia and the Napoleonic Wars

Frederick the Great's younger brother, Prince Augustus William, and his wife, Princess Luise Amalie of Brunswick-Wolfenbüttel, welcomed their son, Frederick William, into the world in 1744. He came to the throne in 1786 at the age of forty-one and was immediately cast in the shadow of his predecessor. Frederick William II moved away from the strict regime of his uncle, which was welcomed by many. Yet, the administration of the kingdom was steered into carelessness and neglect. It is almost certain that whoever followed Frederick the Great on the throne would be compared to him and fall short. However, Frederick William was noted for his love of theater, art, gossip, and his mistresses, as well as his disinterest in listening to his ministers or taking an active part in governing Prussia.

At the end of the 18ᵗʰ century, Prussia's societal dynamics were beginning to shift. The population was still largely peasants with a small number of nobles, but the gradual development of trade and early industrial activity contributed to the emergence of a modest middle class. Frederick the Great had promoted a centralized, bureaucratic state and did not actively support middle-class political influence. Frederick William proved to be a weaker monarch. He was unable to provide consistent leadership in response to these changes. His government moved away from enlightened absolutism, reverting to a more bureaucratic authoritarianism with a focus on maintaining control and stability.

Frederick William had been forced into a marriage with Princess Elisabeth Christine of Brunswick-Wolfenbüttel (not the same Elisabeth Christine who was married to Frederick the Great), which resulted in one daughter. His second marriage to Princess Frederica Louisa of Hesse-Darmstadt produced seven children, including the future Frederick William III. His first mistress, Wilhelmine Enke, was a commoner and the daughter of a horn player in the royal orchestra. He had five children with her. He ended his physical relationship with Wilhelmine several years before taking the throne, but she remained a close companion and confidant. In 1794, he raised her from commoner status to the countess of Lichtenau. He continued several other affairs, including two with the queen's ladies-in-waiting, Julie von Voss and Countess Sophie Dönhoff.

Wilhelmine introduced Frederick William to architect Carl Gotthard Langhans, who would go on to design the famous Brandenburg Gate. Berlin breathed new life with the ascendancy of a new monarch. Germans took the place of Frenchmen in the Academy of the Sciences. Immanuel Kant, a native Prussian, continued publishing, as did Johann Georg Hamann and Johann Gottfried Herder. Literary and scientific clubs grew, not just in the capital but also throughout the kingdom.

The Brandenburg Gate.[17]

Frederick William left foreign policy largely in the hands of Count Hertzberg, who had served faithfully under his uncle. Hertzberg worked under the traditional view that Austria and the Habsburgs were the great enemies of Prussia. However, after a series of diplomatic maneuvers, the death of Emperor Joseph II, and the outbreak of revolution in France in 1789, Hertzberg's power waned. When Frederick William became more involved, the two were often at odds.

The need for a common front against revolutionary France led to the unlikely alliance of Austria and Prussia, which was concluded in 1791. They agreed to war against France, in which Prussia promised to provide twenty thousand men, although it initially sent many more. Russia took this opportunity to invade Poland in the hopes of territorial gain. Prussia and Russia had reached an understanding (of which Austria was unaware at the time), and Prussia also invaded Poland in 1793, capturing Danzig, among other prizes. The Poles mounted a brave defense but were ultimately crushed in 1795.

Meanwhile, the war with France made little headway. Despite popular assumptions, the people of France did not view Prussian, Austrian, or Imperial forces as liberators. The French continually pushed the allies back, and the Prussian coffers that Frederick the Great had left full began to empty. Frederick William's health declined rapidly while he was cared for by his first love, Wilhelmine Enke. He died at the age of fifty-three on November 16th, 1797. His son, Frederick William III, ascended to the throne. He was twenty-seven years old.

Educated under the guidance of his father's court and the values of his great-uncle Frederick the Great, Frederick William III was a more prudent ruler than his father. Despite his great-uncle's religious skepticism, he was instructed by religiously minded teachers. He would remain devout his whole life. In 1793, he met Princess Louise of Mecklenburg-Strelitz. This was one of the few love matches of the Hohenzollern dynasty. While Frederick William III was reserved, she was outgoing. They complemented each other perfectly. They had nine children together.

Frederick William immediately cut royal expenditures upon gaining the throne. He dismissed his father's ministers. But while he certainly had determination, he lacked the trust in his advisors to delegate responsibilities. This severely undermined the effectiveness of his administration.

It was not long into his reign that the rise of Napoleon led to the Napoleonic Wars, which started in 1803. Frederick William and his advisors wished to remain neutral in the conflict. However, the queen believed Prussia must join the other European forces to stop Napoleon, who had crowned himself emperor, from gaining any more power. Prussia was drawn into the conflict in 1806 and joined in the twin battles of Jena and Auerstedt in October of that year. The French decimated the Prussian Army. The Prussians had superior numbers, but their casualties were almost four times those of the French. They were unable to react to the speed and decisiveness of Napoleon's armies. The French then defeated the reserve army and marched into Berlin.

When Napoleon entered Berlin, one of his first stops was to the tomb of Frederick the Great in Potsdam. "Gentlemen," he told the generals gathered around him, "if this man were still alive, I would not be here." In peace negotiations, Napoleon demanded that Prussia give up all its territory west of the River Elbe. Frederick William was willing to agree to these terms, but then Napoleon changed his mind and demanded that Prussia allow French troops to use Prussian lands as a staging ground for an invasion of Russia. In a rare moment of decisiveness, Frederick William rejected the offer.

The royal household was now in Königsberg with the French Army at their heels. Napoleon began to rally support for his invasion of Russia. He offered Austria the region of Silesia back, but the Habsburgs kept their neutrality. Saxony, however, went to the French side, and the elector was made king under Emperor Napoleon.

In 1807, East Prussia became a theater of war. There, the French had large numbers of troops who lived off the land, damaging the common people's farms and crops. Napoleon was able to push the Russians back to Lithuania. Then, at Preussisch-Eylau, Napoleon fought a bloody and indecisive battle against the Russians, who had support from Prussian forces. Although Napoleon was not defeated outright, it was one of his first serious setbacks. However, the Russians did not press their advantage, and Napoleon was able to slip away and regroup.

The Prussian king, now advised by ministers like Karl August von Hardenberg (his chancellor and chief reformer who had modernized Prussia after the 1806 defeat), refused the offer. Napoleon pressed on, gaining control over much of Silesia and Pomerania. Prussia secured alliances with Sweden, Russia, and Great Britain. The terms of the Russian agreement stated the aim was to push the French back across the Rhine and to establish a German confederacy to replace the Holy Roman Empire, with Austria and Prussia as equal powers.

However, to Frederick William's dismay, Russia concluded a ceasefire with Napoleon. Prussia paid the heaviest price in the resulting Treaty of Tilsit, losing significant territory, including lands west of the Elbe, much of its Polish provinces, and its influence in Saxony. Some of the western provinces were incorporated into the newly created Kingdom of Westphalia, with Napoleon's youngest brother, Jérôme Bonaparte, placed on the throne.

The result of this defeat and humiliation was a renewed desire for reform, which had already been on the minds of many officials. The disaster proved to be the opportunity many had hoped for. It would be known as the Prussian Reform Movement. It was not a revolution but rather a reconstruction from within the existing institutions of the Prussian state.

The reforms were widespread. Royal subjects became citizens, echoing the French Revolution. The state was to be the focal point of the community, and feudal restrictions separating subjects by estate would be abolished. Four main reformers gave progress direction, though many others worked at all levels of government: Baron Heinrich Friedrich Karl vom und zum Stein (chief minister who abolished serfdom), Prince Karl August von Hardenberg (chancellor who continued economic reforms), General Gerhard von Scharnhorst (military reformer who opened the officer corps to merit), and Wilhelm von Humboldt (education minister who founded the University of Berlin).

The foreign-born Baron Stein had served under Frederick the Great. Stein recognized a lack of communication between the various departments in the Prussian government and saw that skilled ministers were reduced to messengers while inexperienced members of the royal cabinet made most of the decisions. He envisioned a centralization of power and the establishment of a council of ministers. Stein was a great follower of Adam Smith and wanted to make guilds accessible to all trades, crafts, and professions.

Stein hit a significant barrier when he proposed to eliminate the royal cabinet. His unwillingness to yield on this issue led to a forced resignation and his departure from Prussia. However, he was invited back, thanks to the work of Hardenberg, returning in 1807. Stein and Hardenberg, who had once been adversaries, joined forces and set their sights on the liberation of serfs in all of Prussia.

The serfs would no longer be tied to a lord and his estate, giving them more opportunities, but they also lost many of their legal protections. The nobility was eager to comply with the change because, under the old system, they were obligated to provide for peasants on their land even if their profits suffered. The new system would allow the landholders to evict tenant farmers without notice and consolidate their holdings to maximize their returns.

Stein worked to allow cities to become more self-governed and made it so that more citizens could become burghers, city residents who held the exclusive right to own property and conduct business. However, many groups remained excluded, including most Jewish people, due in part to prevailing prejudices of the time.

Stein also helped to establish the idea that the various lands under Frederick William III's control would officially be known as "Prussia." This completed the unification of Prussia, which had begun in the days of the Great Elector. Stein made drastic cuts to streamline the government. Fifty percent of all public servants lost their jobs. One of Stein's last acts before leaving office under pressure from Napoleon was to suggest to Frederick William that he should place Wilhelm von Humboldt at the head of the administration of culture and education.

Humboldt had developed a concept of national education whose goal was to produce free men capable of fully developing themselves for the benefit of the state. At the heart of this was the concept of the Volk (the people), which did not originate from Humboldt. The Volk were united not within the borders of a nation but by the German language.

Humboldt's reforms widened the number of people who received an education. He also reorganized the education system to ensure efficiency. He helped found the Frederick Wilhelm University of Berlin. Humboldt accomplished all of this in a little over a year and then left his post due to personal issues with Hardenberg in 1810.

Karl August von Hardenberg was, like Stein, not native to Prussia. In 1810, at the age of sixty, he became the chancellor of the state and was entrusted to conduct Prussia's affairs. Hardenberg was hard on subordinates who dared to disagree with him, which was what led to Humboldt's resignation.

Prussia faced French demands for contributions, so Hardenberg confiscated many church lands and sold them cheaply to pay the French. He abolished most tax exemptions and allowed broader participation in trade with some exceptions, which undermined the authority of the guilds.

The nobility greatly opposed Hardenberg. This opposition was often expressed with blatant antisemitism. Adding to these conservative fears was the Edict Concerning the Rights of the Jews. The result of Hardenberg's edict was that approximately seventy thousand Jews officially became Prussian citizens. In 1812, Hardenberg declared that the Jewish people should have the same rights and duties as any other citizen.

At the same time, the military situation was changing in Prussia. A Hanoverian-born officer in service to Prussia, General Gerhard von Scharnhorst recognized the need for reforms in the army. As director of the Prussian Military Academy, he sought to modernize the army, abolish the recruitment of foreigners, end corporal punishment, and limit advancement based on seniority in favor of a system based on merit.

Scharnhorst believed in opening the commissioned ranks to members of the middle class and advocated a shift toward a citizen army rather than an aristocratic professional force. In the aftermath of Prussia's defeat and the imposition of a forty-two-thousand-man cap on its standing army, he introduced the Krümpersystem, under which recruits were rapidly trained, cycled out, and replaced, creating a large reservoir of trained manpower beyond the treaty limit. He also supported the creation of a militia (later the Landwehr), laying the foundation for a broader national defense based on compulsory, universal-style service, though full universal conscription was legally formalized only later.

Scharnhorst purged the senior officers. Of the 143 generals who were active in 1806, only a few remained after he had finished. Corporal punishment was abolished. Training became more focused on the field and the rifle range instead of the parade grounds.

Frederick William III did not turn a blind eye to these reforms. He let men like Hardenberg, Stein, Humboldt, and Scharnhorst do as they wished but only to a point. He recognized the need for reforms, but like his predecessors, he was cautious of political upheaval. His fear was unfounded. If the reforms did anything, it was to instill in the middle class a sense of patriotism and duty to the state, which curbed any influence of revolutionaries. The king remained in power, while the middle class was able to expand its own power and gain more control of the government.

Prussia remained a buffer state between France and Russia, its independence severely limited. Frederick William was required to pay a substantial indemnity, which resulted in the creation of the general income tax. To the surprise of the French, Spain rose in a unified revolt against Napoleon's power. Many hoped that a similar spirit would be raised in Germany. Austria made attempts to ally with Prussia to oppose the usurper. Frederick William would not agree to an alliance unless Russia was involved, and at the moment, Russia was not interested in a war with France.

Due to the revolt in Spain, Napoleon was forced to withdraw several troops from Prussia. In 1809, Austria declared war on France. In Prussia, Stein had been forced to resign under pressure from Napoleon, who saw him as an agitator. Scharnhorst counseled Frederick to declare war on France, as did Queen Louise. Major Ferdinand von Schill from the Prussian Army took it upon himself to wage a campaign against Napoleon, but he was found and killed in May of 1809. Not long after this, Austria signed a peace treaty with France.

It was clear that attitudes were changing, and it soon became apparent that Russia and France were on the brink of war. The French-imposed Continental System had strained Russia's economy, cutting off vital trade with Britain. Though initially aligned with Napoleon, Tsar Alexander grew increasingly uneasy, especially as French influence crept eastward through the reconstitution of a Polish state under French protection. Russia viewed the Duchy of Warsaw as a direct threat to its borders. At the same time, mutual distrust deepened. Napoleon suspected the Russians would abandon the alliance, while Alexander resented France's overreach. As Russia began to loosen its enforcement of the trade blockade, relations further deteriorated. War seemed inevitable, and both sides quietly began to prepare. Frederick William offered an agreement to the French but sent Scharnhorst on a mission to St. Petersburg to conclude a secret alliance there.

Napoleon amassed an army of over 600,000 men for his invasion of Russia in 1812. A significant portion of these forces were Germans. Napoleon advanced, but the Russians pulled back. His army was swallowed by the vastness of Russia. The Russians burned crops as they went, leaving nothing for Napoleon's forces to eat. The French were finally forced to retreat after a few costly victories. This was when the Russians began to truly attack Napoleon's retreating forces.

Prussian soldiers captured by the Russians sometimes joined anti-French units, including the so-called German Legion, which was supported by ex-minister Stein. The Prussian forces in East Prussia were under the command of General Yorck. He continually offered to coordinate with the Russians. He even sent messages to Frederick William to direct him, but the monarchy was, as ever, vacillating. Yorck took it upon himself to sign the Convention of Tauroggen in December 1812, allying with the Russians and beginning the War of Liberation.

It was now 1813. The beloved Queen Louise had been dead for three years. Though Frederick William viewed Yorck's actions as insubordinate, he did not charge the general, and he went along with the Russian alliance. In fact, he seemed invigorated by the new war. He created the Order of the Iron Cross, issued his famous "An Mein Volk" ("To My People") proclamation, and universal conscription was put into place. All of Prussia became unified in their desire to defeat Napoleon and reclaim their country. One of the volunteer units made a point of being German and not purely Prussian. Their uniform of black, red piping, and gold buttons later came to be associated with the German national colors—black, red, and gold.

In August of 1813, Austria joined the Allies. Three Coalition armies converged on Leipzig: the Austrian Army of Bohemia under Field Marshal Karl Philipp Schwarzenberg, the Swedish Army of the North under Crown Prince Charles John, and the Prussian Army of Silesia under Field Marshal Gebhard Leberecht von Blücher.

Blücher was seventy-one years old and had returned to active service when Prussia rejoined the war against Napoleon. A career soldier who had risen through the ranks on merit rather than noble birth, he embodied the spirit of Prussia's military reforms. Known for his aggressive tactics and unrelenting energy, Blücher had earned the nickname "Marshal Forward" for his tendency to push relentlessly toward the enemy. Where other generals hesitated or waited for perfect conditions, Blücher attacked. This mentality, combined with the tactical brilliance of his chief of staff August von Gneisenau, made him a formidable commander.

The resulting Battle of Leipzig (also called the Battle of the Nations) was waged over four days, from October 16th to 19th. On the first day,

Blücher's army engaged French forces in the northern sector at Möckern, where his troops fought Marshal Marmont's corps in brutal close combat. Though the Prussians took heavy casualties, Blücher's persistence wore down the French defenses. His victory at Möckern prevented Napoleon from concentrating his forces and paved the way for the decisive defeat that followed.

By the final day of battle, Napoleon's position had become untenable. The Coalition armies closed in from all sides, and on October 19th, Blücher's forces stormed Leipzig itself. The battle involved approximately 560,000 soldiers and led to 133,000 casualties, making it the largest battle in European history before World War I. Napoleon was forced to retreat westward, and French dominance over Germany collapsed.

For his role at Leipzig, Blücher was promoted to field marshal and given the title prince of Wahlstatt. He became a hero of Prussia's War of Liberation, a symbol of the nation's resurgence after the humiliations of 1806.

At the Congress of Vienna, which concluded the Napoleonic Wars, Prussia regained its place as a great power. Hardenberg and Humboldt attended the congress. Frederick William was also in Vienna, working behind the scenes. Prussia acquired significant territory, including much of Saxony, parts of the Duchy of Warsaw (Poland), Danzig, and the Grand Duchy of the Lower Rhine, along with other lands lost during the Napoleonic Wars.

Chapter 8: Prussia's Economic and Social Revolution

While the Congress of Vienna restored and expanded Prussia's borders, the country and its people had been rocked by years of war. A complete restoration was needed to pull the country out of the trauma of the turn of the 19th century, and it would not be found in more war or political maneuvers but in economic growth and development. After the Napoleonic Wars, Prussia remained largely agrarian and less industrialized than Britain, which had already entered the Industrial Revolution. Prussia found itself behind the times, but it still benefited from the reforms established years before. It also had one of the most progressive education systems in Europe. This created generations of thinkers, engineers, and entrepreneurs who would utilize everything Prussia had to offer to bring about its own industrial development.

After Napoleon's abdication and exile to Elba, he famously returned and gathered an army, only to be finally defeated at Waterloo in 1815. The two great leaders who faced Napoleon were Lord Wellington of Britain and the aged hero of Leipzig, Prussian Field Marshal Blücher. Napoleon was once again exiled, this time to St. Helena, where he died. With Napoleon defeated, Prussia was able to focus on securing what it had and expanding where it could.

Economic measures were already enacted that promoted trade and cooperation among German states. Though Austria held German provinces, Prussia was increasingly seen as the rightful leader of any

German organization. There was pressure on Frederick William to acknowledge a constitutional monarchy instead of the patchwork absolutism he enjoyed. The king and his allies did everything they could to avoid this.

In 1818, Prussia secured a large loan from the banking house of Rothschild, allowing the government not only to function but also to pursue economic interests and support industrial development. This was especially noticeable in Westphalia. There, the well-traveled provincial president Ludwig von Vincke, an admirer of British self-governance, promoted economic modernization. The newly developed coalfields in the Ruhr became the backbone of Prussia's economic strength.

A road-building program began in the early 19th century and expanded steadily over the next decades. By the late 1840s, Prussia had built a large and growing network of state-owned roads. The railway was also a revolution in the country's transportation system. The first line opened in 1838 between Berlin and Potsdam.

Frederick William III was not impressed. He complained that his peace and quiet were suffering just to be "a few hours earlier to Berlin." However, most of the country welcomed the new speed. By 1844, Prussia had several hundred kilometers of track. Four years later, the total had nearly tripled. In 1840, Prussians began building their own locomotives instead of importing them.

Prussia was outpacing many smaller German states economically. For example, while pig-iron and steel production in regions like Saxony remained modest in the 1830s, Prussia, aided by its mineral resources, was quickly scaling up output across multiple smelters. One significant case was the firm now known as Krupp. Alfred Krupp dropped out of school to manage his family's failing steelworks at the age of fourteen, inheriting the secret of producing high-quality cast steel. Over the following decades, as demand for steel for railways and industrial machinery surged, Krupp's business turned a profit. The quality of his cast steel proved so high that by the 1850s and 1860s, he began producing artillery. He eventually supplied weapons to many countries and earned the nickname "The Cannon King." From humble beginnings, he built a massive industrial fortune and established a foundation for Prussia's—and later Germany's—steel armaments dominance.

August Borsig (1804–1854), the son of a carpenter from Silesia, started his industrial career with limited capital. Borsig initially built equipment for sugar refineries but soon transitioned to the manufacture of locomotive parts. In 1840, he built his first complete locomotive, which performed as well as the English-made engines being imported into the country at the time. He eventually opened additional works to supply the increased demand for trains. At the time of his death in 1854, he had built several hundred locomotives. By 1872, his company had become one of the largest producers of locomotives in Europe.

Steam engines had first been introduced to Prussia in the 18th century, but it was in the 19th century that they saw widespread use. By the 1830s, steam power had begun to transform factories, mines, and workshops across the kingdom. In the west, Prussia's newly acquired territories along the Rhine (gained at the Congress of Vienna in 1815) proved economically vital. Prussia's coal-rich regions became the center of this early industrial shift. The Saar region, which had once been under Napoleon's control but was now part of the Prussian Rhineland, saw sharp increases in coal output through the 1820s and 1830s. The Ruhr Valley, also part of these western acquisitions, saw production expand rapidly after 1815, helped by improved mining techniques and rising demand for fuel. These regions would soon become the heart of Prussia's heavy industry. Steam power and coal were laying the foundations of a new industrial economy.

Industrialization required not just laborers but also skilled engineers and technicians. To answer this need, the Royal Technical Institute (a predecessor of the Technical University of Berlin) was established in 1821. To demonstrate Prussia's advancements to an international audience, exhibitions were organized in 1822, 1827, and 1844.

As is so often the case, those who suffered the most from industrialization were those at the bottom of the social hierarchy. The Stein-Hardenberg reforms had done much to help the middle class, but they had led to many peasants losing their small landholdings, as the nobility was able to evict tenant farmers more freely. Peasants who managed to retain their small holdings could not compete with the large-scale farmers around them and had to sell their land and move to cities to become factory workers.

Conditions at Prussia's factories were notably bad. Workdays were long and dangerous, with little time off. Child labor was rampant. The government's solution of setting a minimum age of nine for workers did little to help the issue. It would take several more decades before workers were given a voice.

Interestingly, the arts prospered at this time. Gottfried von Schadow, the famous sculptor of the chariot and four horses atop the Brandenburg Gate, had a pupil named Christian Daniel Rauch (1777–1857). Rauch completed several noteworthy works in the early 19th century, including a statue of sleeping Queen Louise, which was placed in her mausoleum. It is a defining piece of neoclassical sculpture in Prussia. Rauch also sculpted monuments to Blücher and Scharnhorst, as well as a colossal equestrian statue of Frederick the Great, which is today considered a masterpiece of the Berlin school of sculpture and marks a transition to realism in the capital.

Queen Louise of Prussia by Christian Daniel Rauch.[18]

Gottfried Schadow's son, Friedrich Wilhelm Schadow (1789–1862), and Alfred Rethel (1816–1859) were both well-known German painters. Schadow is perhaps better known as a teacher and Rethel for his historical paintings, drawings, and eccentric character. Felix Mendelssohn (1809–1847) moved with his family as a young child to Berlin and eventually studied under German composers Ludwig Berger and Carl Friedrich Zelter. A prolific composer from an early age, Felix composed thirteen string symphonies between the ages of twelve and fourteen. Mendelssohn was favorably compared to Mozart. In 1833, he was made musical director at Düsseldorf. He then moved to Leipzig and eventually Britain.

Great thinkers like Georg Wilhelm Friedrich Hegel (1770–1831) also lived at this time. Hegel held the chair of philosophy at the University of Berlin from 1818 until his death. There were well-known female thinkers as well. Bettina von Arnim was a German Romantic author and composer. Her most famous books were reworkings of correspondence with real people.

Rahel Varnhagen (1771–1833), the daughter of a Jewish merchant, was born in Berlin and went on to host one of the most prominent salons in the late 18th and early 19th centuries. She is remembered for her vast amount of correspondence and the famous intellectuals who came to her salon, including the Humboldt brothers, Wilhelm and Alexander.

Wilhelm von Humboldt was, of course, a minister and diplomat, but he was also a philosopher. His studies of languages, particularly Basque, remain influential to this day. Wilhelm's younger brother, Alexander (1769–1859), is remembered as a leader in botanical and geographic studies. Between 1799 and 1804, he traveled extensively in the Americas and wrote about his journey over the course of several years and twenty-one volumes. Other luminaries include the historian Leopold von Ranke and jurist and historian Friedrich Carl von Savigny. Karl Marx might have joined them if he had not been denied a lectureship at Berlin University.

The political climate of Prussia was charged in the 1830s. Tensions rose between the government and the Catholic Church when a dispute broke out between the church and the Prussian government over the terms under which mixed Catholic-Protestant marriages could be recognized by the Catholic Church. This had been accepted by previous bishops under pressure, but the new archbishop of Cologne refused to comply with the state's terms. At the same time, constitutionalists were agitating for a constitutional monarchy.

On January 7th, 1840, Frederick William III died. The throne passed to his son, Frederick William IV.

The younger Frederick had been his mother's favorite son. When she died when he was only fourteen years old, the prince saw it as a punishment from God. He had been a child when his family was forced to flee the approaching French soldiers, and like many royalty who lived during the French Revolution, he feared the power of the mob might topple his own power. As crown prince, he did not care for the reforms of Stein and Hardenberg. He fought in the Wars of Liberation that drove the French out of Germany. He became a Romanticist with a nostalgic view of the Middle Ages.

Frederick William IV's accession to the throne was cheered by the population at large. Many liberals who had gone into exile were welcomed back, including the famous Brothers Grimm. (The Grimms had been among the "Göttingen Seven," professors who had been dismissed and exiled from Hanover in 1837 for protesting the king's abolition of the constitution.) Alexander von Humboldt was appointed state councilor. However, the king also appointed his close friends to high positions, men who were conservatives with the religious fervor of Pietist revivalism. Many wondered if Frederick William would be a liberal or a Pietist monarch, but in truth, the king wanted to be both.

He delivered public speeches, something his father had never done. However, his words bordered on religious sermons with little political value. Many liberals came to believe he was not a man of action as they had hoped. The king's concept of monarchy was fundamentally different from that of many of his ancestors. He did not see himself as the first servant of the state but instead believed he held his crown by the grace of God. He deeply trusted in the power of divine will, and this led to inaction at important moments.

Frederick William IV supported the "German" cause to return Germany to its medieval splendor, but he appeared not to realize that this would mean losing his kingdom to a German emperor. He eased the troubles between the state and the Roman Catholic Church. He believed this was the first step toward reconciliation between Catholics and Protestants. He also restarted the building of the Cologne Cathedral.

In 1843 and 1844, the cotton market was depressed, and the weavers of Silesia were hit particularly hard. The Silesian weavers' protest of 1844 reflected growing hardship and discontent in the industrial working class.

In 1847, after years of economic woes and bad harvests, several revolts broke out in Prussia. King Frederick William IV had tried to avoid constitutionalism, but the crises of his country forced his hand. On February 3rd, 1847, he published a decree that created the United Diet, a legislative assembly. This assembly would meet when summoned by the king for matters such as approving new taxes or loans. However, the decree seemed too little, too late.

In 1848, the Second French Republic was proclaimed, and a tide of revolution swept through Europe. It began in Cologne on March 3rd, 1848, with a mass demonstration of workers, which spread through the Rhineland. Frederick William tried again to appeal to the people's liberal demands, but his proclamations fell short of expectations. The German intelligentsia met in Heidelberg in March of 1848 and resolved to press for a German, not a Prussian, national assembly. They wanted a German constitution and for a preliminary parliament, the Vorparlament, to be convened that month in Frankfurt am Main. They resolved to maintain the freedom of the press and adopted the national colors of black, red, and gold.

On March 18th, thousands gathered outside the royal palace in Berlin. The crowd demanded reforms: a constitution, freedom of the press, civil liberties, and Prussia's leadership in creating a unified German nation. The king addressed the crowd and appeared to promise reforms, but tensions remained high.

As troops attempted to clear the palace square, two shots rang out. Whether they were fired accidentally or deliberately remains disputed. In the chaos that followed, soldiers opened fire on the crowd. The violence continued through the afternoon and into the evening, with hundreds of civilians killed or wounded. Bodies were carried through the streets, and fury at the military spread throughout Berlin.

Open revolt broke out. The revolutionaries, made up of the working class, students, artisans, and burghers, erected over a thousand barricades throughout the city. Street fighting continued through the night of March 18th. Military leaders advised the king to both flee the city and crush the rebellion with overwhelming force. Frederick William instead issued another proclamation, asking the Berliners to return peacefully to their homes. When this proved ineffective, he made a fateful decision. He ordered troops to withdraw from the inner city. Amid the confusion, the revolutionaries celebrated what appeared to be a victory.

The king's brother, Prince William of Prussia, whom many held responsible for ordering the troops to fire on March 18th, fled the country in disguise, eventually reaching England. The revolutionaries formed a citizen militia to maintain order and prevent looting. In response to continued demands for reform, Frederick William appeared before crowds wearing a black, red, and gold sash—the colors of German liberalism and unification. He famously declared, "Prussia henceforth merges with Germany." Still, the Prussian government was in disarray, and the statement remained largely rhetorical.

The primary issue of a unified German state was the question of who would be at its head. The major German powers were Prussia and Austria. The men at the Frankfurt convention wanted a broad German Empire headed by a hereditary royal family but governed by a constitution. The Habsburgs of Austria refused to participate because they rejected constitutionalism and ruled over many non-German provinces.

A "lesser Germany," excluding Austrian lands and placing Frederick William IV as German emperor, was proposed. However, Frederick would not accept the convention's terms. He had no interest in their constitution and remained opposed to democratization in his kingdom. New revolts broke out, and this time, Frederick responded with force. The revolutions were violently suppressed. The Revolution of 1848 had failed.

The Frankfurt Parliament had grand ambitions, but it was too divided and lacked real power. Western Europe viewed the revolution warily. A unified Germany, potentially stretching from the North Sea to the Black Sea, was seen as a major threat to the balance of power. France was prepared to ally with Russia to suppress it. Britain, while sympathetic to liberal ideas, opposed a strong German central power.

Things returned, for the most part, to the status quo, but the whole of Germany—and especially Prussia—had been greatly shaken. Many Germans turned away from revolutionary politics. What did not subside was the steady progress of industrialization. Prussia saw a substantial increase in the use of steam engines during the mid-19th century, although exact figures vary. Germany's railway network expanded rapidly, covering thousands of kilometers by the 1860s.

Mechanization gradually replaced artisans, and factories grew larger. Textile manufacturing became increasingly mechanized during this period. The textile sector underwent consolidation, resulting in a decrease in the number of companies. Industry continued to expand, with shareholding companies growing rapidly, particularly in railways, mining, steel, iron, banks, and insurance. Prussia, and to a greater extent Germany, was on the verge of great change.

Chapter 9: German Unification

In 1847, a thirty-two-year-old Junker nobleman from an estate near Schönhausen married Johanna von Puttkamer and gained social and financial stability that supported his entry into public life. That same year, he became a representative in the newly created Prussian United Diet. He made a name for himself as an ultra-conservative royalist, but it also became clear that he was a capable politician who quickly learned to maneuver through the evolving legislative system of his country. Initially, when he entered Prussian politics, he opposed German unification, believing it would compromise Prussia's independence.

His strong support for the monarchy did not go unnoticed. In 1851, King Frederick William IV appointed him as Prussia's representative to the German Confederate Diet in Frankfurt. This envoy's name was Otto von Bismarck, and he would come to be considered the architect of the German Empire.

Born in 1815, Bismarck was the son of a landowning Junker and former Prussian military officer. His mother was the daughter of a senior government official. He spent much of his youth between the family estates in Schönhausen and Kniephof (in Farther Pomerania, now part of Poland). He was well educated and had knowledge of several languages, including English, French, and Russian. He studied law at the University of Göttingen in Lower Saxony and then at the University of Berlin from 1833 to 1835.

Bismarck later undertook a period of agricultural study while managing the family estate and serving in the Landwehr (the Prussian reserve army). He had hoped for a diplomatic career, but his early civil service posts were short-lived. Though regarded as eccentric in his youth, he displayed considerable charm and intelligence, traits that later served him well in politics.

After his mother's death in the early 1840s, Bismarck returned home to manage the family estate. He later became engaged to Johanna, whom he knew through her cousin, who was married to one of his close friends. Johanna was known to be quiet and modest but also sharp-witted. With their marriage, Bismarck's political career began in earnest with his 1847 election to the United Diet. The following year, a revolution broke out in Prussia.

While King Frederick William IV was making concessions to the revolutionaries, Bismarck, in his role as a loyal monarchist, reportedly tried to persuade the king's sister-in-law, Augusta, to support replacing the king with her son, Prince Frederick William. She refused. The liberal revolutionaries were eventually divided by internal conflicts, and conservatives regained power, promising reforms but ultimately preserving much of the existing political structure.

In 1849, Bismarck was elected to the Prussian Landtag (the lower house of Parliament). He remained generally opposed to the liberal nationalist vision of German unification, though he accepted an appointment as a Prussian delegate to the Erfurt Union Parliament in 1850—a short-lived attempt by Prussia and several smaller German states to unify Germany without Austria. Bismarck attended in order to safeguard Prussian interests, not to promote unification, and the effort soon collapsed.

In 1851, Bismarck was appointed Prussian envoy to the Diet of the German Confederation in Frankfurt. There, he frequently clashed with the Austrian representative, Friedrich von Thun und Hohenstein, and insisted on equal treatment, such as the right to smoke or remove his jacket during sessions. One notable incident resulted in a duel with fellow Prussian deputy Georg von Vincke; neither party was injured.

Bismarck spent eight years in Frankfurt, during which his political views evolved. Distanced from the Prussian court, he began to adopt a more pragmatic approach. He came to believe that Prussia needed to form alliances with other German states in order to challenge Austrian dominance, and his thinking on unification began to shift. He increasingly felt that both conservatives and moderate liberals could support a German unification that preserved the traditional social order under Prussian leadership.

Bismarck disapproved of Prussia's neutral stance during the Crimean War and believed the kingdom should maintain a close alliance with Russia while keeping ties with Napoleon III's France. In 1857, King Frederick William IV suffered a debilitating stroke, and his brother Wilhelm became regent. Wilhelm, seen as a moderate conservative, started the so-called "New Era," implementing changes in leadership and policy direction. Bismarck was removed from his post in Frankfurt and reassigned as ambassador to Russia. Though this was technically a promotion, Bismarck felt sidelined from developments in Germany.

Nevertheless, during his four-year posting in St. Petersburg, Bismarck remained informed about Prussian affairs, thanks in part to his close relationship with Albrecht von Roon, the minister of war. Roon, along with General Helmuth von Moltke, shared Bismarck's conservative yet pragmatic outlook. The three men would become the central figures in the drive for German unification under Prussian leadership.

In 1861, King Frederick William IV died, and his brother ascended the throne as King Wilhelm (or William) I. Frederick William IV had said in his will that he hoped Wilhelm would repeal the constitution, but Wilhelm ignored his dead brother's wishes. He inherited a government strained from the tension between the Landtag and the monarchy.

In 1862, a crisis arose in which the legislature refused to approve a military spending increase to reorganize the Prussian Army. King Wilhelm threatened to abdicate in favor of his son, who was believed to be more liberal. However, Albrecht von Roon was able to convince the king that the only person capable of handling the crisis was Otto von Bismarck. Bismarck was recalled, and Wilhelm appointed him minister president and foreign minister.

Despite the king's misgivings about Bismarck, Otto soon had a powerful hold on the monarchy. He desired to maintain the power of the monarchy above all else, and he looked for a way around the current crisis. The constitution stated that a budget must be approved by the legislature and the monarchy, but it did not specify what to do in the case of a deadlock. Bismarck argued that the previous year's budget could be used to keep the government functioning by the continuation of tax collection, thus avoiding catastrophe.

Bismarck focused on German unification, envisioning Prussia as the leading entity in a German nation. In 1862, he delivered an often-quoted speech in which he said that unification would not be won with speeches and majority decisions but with iron and blood. However, his censorship of the press made him generally unpopular, and the liberal legislature demanded that the king dismiss him. The crown prince opposed Bismarck, and the queen continued to dislike him after how he had acted during the 1848 revolution. However, this did nothing to dissuade the king from believing that Prussia would only prevail with the aid of Bismarck.

Prussia's circumstances changed with the death of King Frederick VII of Denmark in 1863. The Danish king died without a direct heir, triggering a succession crisis over the duchies of Schleswig and Holstein. These territories occupied a complicated position. Holstein was predominantly German-speaking and a member of the German Confederation, while Schleswig had mixed Danish and German populations. Both were ruled by the Danish king, but they were not incorporated into Denmark itself.

The succession question had been temporarily settled by the London Protocol of 1852, which designated Prince Christian of Glücksburg as heir to both the Danish throne and the duchies, but it required the duchies to remain separate from Denmark proper. However, when Christian ascended as King Christian IX in November 1863, he immediately signed the November Constitution, which integrated Schleswig directly into the Danish kingdom. This was a clear violation of the 1852 agreement.

Bismarck saw an opportunity. He convinced Austria to join Prussia in demanding that Denmark reverse the constitution. When Denmark refused, Bismarck had his justification for war. In February 1864, Prussian and Austrian forces invaded, beginning what became known as the Second Schleswig War.

Austrian and Prussian troops entered Schleswig in February 1864. The Danish troops were outnumbered and poorly led, facing grueling retreats amid harsh winter conditions. Danish attempts to block invasion routes proved unsuccessful.

The Prussians continued to push through Schleswig, and military operations extended into Jutland. This had not been part of the original plan, but Bismarck improvised and convinced the Austrians of the need for force to settle the question of the provinces and the German Confederation for good. The war continued into the summer. Attempts were made to come to a ceasefire, but the negotiations often fell apart. By July, most of Jutland had been occupied by the German forces. Only the Danish islands remained.

In October 1864, after agreeing to abandon claims to the duchies, Denmark signed the Treaty of Vienna. Denmark handed over Schleswig, Holstein, and the Duchy of Lauenburg to the Prussians and Austrians. By giving away these provinces, the Danes lost roughly 40 percent of their land area and about one million citizens.

Prussia came out of the conflict as the superior force. The reorganization of their army proved more than effective, and this led the other nations of the German Confederation to see Prussia as the only country able to protect a unified Germany from outside aggression. Prussia and Austria agreed to administer Schleswig and Holstein jointly, but Bismarck was clearly already envisioning the duchies as part of the German nation without the Austrians' involvement.

The joint Austro-Prussian victory immediately created a new problem: what to do with the conquered territories. Both powers claimed rights to the duchies, but neither could agree on their future status. Should they become independent German states? Be annexed directly? Given to a German prince? The two victors spent months in tense negotiations.

Finally, in August 1865, they reached a compromise in the Convention of Gastein. Austria would administer Holstein, Prussia would govern Schleswig, Lauenburg would be sold to Prussia (for 2.5 million Danish rigsdaler), and both powers would jointly control the strategic port city of Kiel. This arrangement satisfied no one. It merely postponed the inevitable confrontation between the two German powers. The joint administration was awkward and unworkable from the start, with each power suspicious of the other's intentions in their respective zones.

In January 1866, a crisis erupted between the two powers that governed Schleswig-Holstein. The Austrian governor of Holstein had permitted the estates to call up a general assembly. Prussia protested this decision, saying that it undermined its authority. Austria countered that this was not true, but not wanting to take any chances, they reinforced their troops along their border with Prussia.

In April, Bismarck secured a crucial alliance with Italy. The newly unified Italian kingdom still lacked Veneto, the wealthy northeastern province that remained under Austrian control. Bismarck promised that if Italy joined Prussia in a war against Austria, Veneto would be theirs. Italy agreed, and Austria immediately mobilized its southern army along the Italian border. By May, all three powers had mobilized, making war inevitable.

Austria attempted to use its traditional leadership position in German affairs to isolate Prussia. In June, Austria brought formal charges against Prussia before both the Frankfurt Diet of the German Confederation and the Holstein Diet, accusing Prussia of violating the Convention of Gastein and threatening German unity. Prussia's response was dramatic. Bismarck declared the joint administration of Schleswig-Holstein null and void, and Prussian troops marched into Holstein, expelling the Austrian garrison.

The German Confederation immediately called for mobilization against Prussia, voting to place federal troops under Austrian command. Most of the German states, including Saxony, Hanover, Bavaria, Württemberg, Baden, and Hesse-Kassel, sided with Austria, viewing Prussian aggression as a threat to the traditional German order. Only a handful of smaller northern states joined Prussia.

Bismarck declared the German Confederation, an institution that had existed since 1815, dissolved, and Prussian armies immediately invaded Saxony, Hanover, and Hesse-Kassel before they could fully mobilize. The Austro-Prussian War, which would determine the future shape of Germany, had begun.

Years later, Bismarck would claim he had orchestrated the entire crisis with a calculated view toward German unification under Prussian leadership and even with an eye toward an eventual confrontation with France that would complete that unification.

Some suggest that Bismarck was embellishing his intentions for his later aggrandizement. Some historians argue that Bismarck was a Prussian expansionist and only nominally committed to the idea of German unification. His alliance with Austria had been to gain control of Schleswig-Holstein, and his later turn against the Austrians was to secure the duchies for Prussia alone. Of course, it is impossible to know with complete certainty. What is certain is that Bismarck's actions led directly to the declaration of war between Austria, Prussia, some of the German states, and Italy.

The war that would determine Germany's future lasted just seven weeks, earning it the nickname the "Seven Weeks' War." Prussian forces quickly overwhelmed their opponents. In the north, Hanoverian forces resisted stubbornly but were defeated at Langensalza on June 27th and forced to surrender two days later. Prussian columns swept through Saxony, Hesse-Kassel, and other states that had sided with Austria, facing little organized resistance.

The decisive campaign unfolded in Bohemia. Austrian forces under Ludwig von Benedek assembled a massive army—over 200,000 men— supported by Saxon contingents. The Prussian armies, divided into three separate columns under the overall command of Field Marshal Helmuth von Moltke, converged on the Austrian position near the fortress town of Königgrätz (modern-day Hradec Králové in the Czech Republic).

On July 3rd, the two armies clashed in one of the largest recorded battles in Europe. Nearly half a million soldiers fought across a twelve-mile front. The battle hung in the balance for hours until the Prussian Second Army, commanded by Crown Prince Frederick William, arrived on the Austrian right flank in the afternoon. Caught in a pincer, Austrian forces broke and retreated in disorder, suffering over forty thousand casualties to Prussia's nine thousand. It was a catastrophic defeat that shattered Austrian military power.

Meanwhile, on the Italian front, the war went less smoothly for Prussia's ally. Despite numerical superiority, Italian forces were defeated by the Austrians at Custoza on June 24th and in a naval battle at Lissa in the Adriatic on July 20th. However, these Austrian victories came too late. Königgrätz had already decided the war, and Austria was forced to divide its armies between two fronts, fatally weakening the Bohemian campaign.

Prussia's rapid victory stemmed from several advantages. The Prussian Army was equipped with the Dreyse needle gun, a breech-loading rifle that could fire five times faster than the Austrian muzzle-loaders and could be loaded while prone, giving Prussian infantry devastating firepower. Even more important was Prussia's railway network, which allowed Moltke to mobilize and concentrate armies with unprecedented speed. While Austrian troops were still marching toward concentration points, Prussian forces had already deployed via rail and invaded enemy territory.

By late July, Bismarck faced a delicate situation. Prussia had won decisively, but King Wilhelm I and the Prussian generals wanted to march on Vienna and impose a humiliating peace on Austria. Bismarck vehemently opposed this. He feared that France, which had been watching the war nervously, might intervene if Prussia appeared too threatening. More importantly, Bismarck wanted Austria weakened but not destroyed. He still saw Austria as a potential future ally and wanted to avoid creating lasting enmity. After fierce arguments with the king and military leadership, Bismarck prevailed.

The Peace of Prague, signed on August 23rd, 1866, was surprisingly lenient to Austria. Austria paid no indemnity and ceded no territory to Prussia. Only Veneto went to Italy, which was transferred through French mediation to save Austrian pride. However, the treaty's political consequences were revolutionary. Austria was permanently excluded from German affairs, ending centuries of Habsburg leadership. The German Confederation was formally dissolved. Prussia annexed Schleswig-Holstein, Hanover, Hesse-Kassel, Nassau, and Frankfurt, growing dramatically in size and population. The remaining German states north of the Main River were organized into a new North German Confederation under Prussian dominance, while the southern states (Bavaria, Württemberg, Baden, and Hesse-Darmstadt) remained independent but were forced into secret military alliances with Prussia.

In seven weeks, Bismarck had fundamentally reordered Germany. Austria was expelled, Prussia was the dominant power, and the path toward German unification under Prussian leadership was clear.

The Hanoverians proved especially resistant to annexation. Their king, King George V, protested along with the population. Prince Frederick William of Hesse-Kassel condemned the annexation and the end of the Electorate of Hesse. A strong anti-Prussian undercurrent continued for years afterward, disrupting Prussia's plans. Still, the process continued.

The North German Confederation was initially only a military alliance, but within a year of its creation, it had established a federal constitution with the king of Prussia as its monarch. A new parliament was created, called the Reichstag, based on universal male suffrage. A combined conservative and liberal coalition worked to establish a Northern German system of government.

Bismarck had, seemingly against all odds, accomplished exactly what he set out to do. He was not loved by his countrymen or even well liked. He was often at odds with fellow ministers and even the king, but he had made himself indispensable. And that power had upended the order of power in the German Confederation. Austria was not only no longer the superior power, but it was also excluded from German politics completely.

Bismarck's "soft peace" with Austria allowed the two countries to resume stable relations not long after the war. Austria was too concerned with the Italians and pan-Slavic movements to make a lasting enemy of Prussia. The German states, which had largely sided with Austria in the war or had remained neutral, now found themselves yoked to the Prussian wagon. Bismarck did all this even though he commanded no army, led no political party, and was not a member of the royal family. Yet, Bismarck had little time to gloat because larger enemies were just beyond the horizon.

Tensions with the Second Empire of France and Emperor Napoleon III had begun before the ink had dried on the Peace of Prague. Napoleon had hoped that France would gain land in Belgium and along the Rhine as a reward for not joining the war against Prussia, but the war had ended too quickly for him to take advantage of the situation. Bismarck did not necessarily want to avoid war with France, but he was certainly wary. France might find a ready ally in Austria, or Russia might join the war against Prussia. However, if Prussia could defeat France, it would only help to solidify the various German states.

A pretext for war came in 1870 with the question of Spanish succession. When the Spanish throne became vacant, Prince Leopold of the Hohenzollern-Sigmaringen branch was offered the crown. Napoleon III, alarmed at the prospect of Hohenzollern rulers on both his eastern and southern borders, pressured Leopold to withdraw. Leopold complied, but Napoleon III demanded more. He wanted a binding guarantee that no Hohenzollern would ever accept the Spanish throne. Since King Wilhelm of Prussia was the head of the entire House of Hohenzollern, Napoleon sent his ambassador, Count Vincent Benedetti, to meet Wilhelm at the spa town of Ems in July 1870 to extract this humiliating promise.

Wilhelm politely but firmly refused to give such a guarantee and sent Bismarck a telegram describing the meeting. Bismarck saw his opportunity. He edited the telegram to make it appear that Wilhelm had brusquely dismissed the French ambassador and that the ambassador had been insulting to the king. He then released this doctored version (called the Ems Dispatch) to the press on July 13th, 1870. The edited text enraged both nations. The French felt humiliated, and the Germans felt their king had been insulted. Bismarck later admitted he had made the telegram sound "like a red rag to the Gallic bull." France declared war on Prussia on July 19th, 1870.

In the German states, France was seen as the aggressor. German patriotism swelled to face the common foe. Bismarck's concerns about Austrian or Russian involvement proved unfounded, and his belief that war would unify Germans against France was realized. The southern German states—Bavaria, Württemberg, Baden, and Hesse-Darmstadt—honored their secret military alliances with Prussia and sent their armies to join the fight.

The war was a catastrophe for France. Prussian and allied German forces, again benefiting from superior organization, railway mobilization, and the needle gun, won decisive victories at Wissembourg, Spicheren, and Wörth in early August. By September 1st, the main French Army under Marshal MacMahon was trapped at Sedan near the Belgian border. After a day of fierce fighting, with 17,000 French dead and wounded and 104,000 captured, including Napoleon III himself, the French Army surrendered. The emperor was taken prisoner and eventually went into exile in England, where he died in 1873.

However, the war was not over. The French declared a Third Republic and continued fighting under a government of national defense. The French forces under Marshal Bazaine surrendered at Metz in October with 173,000 men. Paris endured a brutal four-month siege through the winter of 1870/71, with civilians reduced to eating rats, cats, and zoo animals as food supplies dwindled. The city finally capitulated in January 1871. The Franco-Prussian War formally ended with the Treaty of Frankfurt in May 1871, which imposed harsh terms. France had to pay a massive indemnity of five billion francs and ceded Alsace and most of Lorraine to Germany. These territories had significant German-speaking populations but also many French speakers. This humiliation would poison Franco-German relations for decades and help sow the seeds of World War I.

Bismarck used the momentum of this military victory to bring about German unification. During the siege of Paris, he negotiated with the southern German states, offering them significant concessions to join the North German Confederation. These included control over their own railways, postal services, and independent military commands in peacetime, as well as special voting arrangements in the Bundesrat, the upper legislative house representing the states, which sat above the popularly elected Reichstag. Bavaria, in particular, received substantial autonomy in return for joining.

On January 18th, 1871, in the Hall of Mirrors at the Palace of Versailles (which was deliberately chosen to humiliate France on its own soil in the very palace built by Louis XIV as a symbol of French grandeur), King Wilhelm of Prussia was proclaimed the first German emperor (Kaiser Wilhelm I). Bismarck became the first chancellor of the German Empire. The ceremony was attended by German princes, military commanders, and officials. The French notably did not attend. They watched helplessly as their historic palace became the birthplace of a unified German state.

The new empire was a federation of twenty-five different states—four kingdoms (Prussia, Bavaria, Württemberg, and Saxony), six grand duchies, five duchies, seven principalities, and three free cities (Hamburg, Bremen, and Lübeck). The emperor was "first among equals" and presided over the Bundesrat. For the first time since the Holy Roman Empire had dissolved in 1806, Germany was united under one government, and that government was led by Prussia.

Chapter 10: End of an Era: Prussia's Dissolution and Legacy

When Wilhelm gained the title of emperor, Otto von Bismarck became the chancellor of the German Empire. He was also raised to the rank of prince. He retained all of his previous offices and gained so many new ones that he was now virtually in control of much of the domestic and foreign policy. Europe entered a period of relative stability among the great powers after 1871, and Bismarck became a leading European figure.

After the Franco-Prussian War, Bismarck supported the annexation of Alsace-Lorraine from France. Many in Germany approved of this. The Prussian Army argued that the territory offered a better defensive frontier. The annexation embittered France, and relations between Germany and Russia also became occasionally strained, although Bismarck worked to maintain a balance of alliances. Germany secured close ties with Austria-Hungary and later Italy.

Bismarck had been largely opposed to German colonization, viewing overseas territories as expensive distractions that could entangle Germany in conflicts with Britain and France. But in 1883, he reversed his stance, and Germany began to acquire overseas colonies in Africa and the South Pacific. Germany joined the Scramble for Africa and acquired territories, including Togoland, Cameroon, German South West Africa (later Namibia), and German East Africa (parts of present-day Tanzania, Rwanda, and Burundi). Bismarck's motives for expanding the German Empire have been debated by historians. Some say he yielded to pressure to keep pace with other European powers, while others claim it was part of his domestic realpolitik.

Throughout his chancellorship, he maintained that he was doing all he could to avoid another European war. His domestic goals moved toward the creation of a welfare state that promoted loyalty to the state and the crown, but he made sure to create welfare programs that would be acceptable to conservatives. He pushed through a bill that provided sickness insurance for German workers; this, along with other state benefits, slowed the tide of Germans emigrating to the United States.

However, Bismarck's total control was shaken with the death of German Emperor Wilhelm I in 1888 after a short illness. He was ninety years old. Wilhelm was succeeded by his son, Frederick, who was already suffering from throat cancer. Frederick III reigned for only ninety-nine days before dying on June 15th, 1888, dashing liberal hopes that he would reform the empire along more constitutional lines. He was succeeded by his son, Wilhelm, who was crowned Emperor Wilhelm II the same day, making 1888 the "Year of the Three Emperors."

Wilhelm II was born on January 27th, 1859. His mother was Victoria, Princess Royal, the eldest daughter of Queen Victoria of Britain. His birth was traumatic, and as a result, he was born with a withered left arm. Some have speculated, though never proven, that he might have also suffered a minor neurological injury. He was the eldest grandson of Queen Victoria, and his parents hoped to give him a liberal British education. However, he was heavily influenced by Prussian culture, which centered around the military and masculinity.

Wilhelm II attended the University of Bonn, where he studied law and politics. On his eighteenth birthday, his grandmother gave him the Order of the Garter. He showed a strong intellect, but this was often overshadowed by his tempestuous demeanor. While he originally worshiped his father, a hero of the wars of unification, he grew to become ambivalent toward both his parents as he came to adulthood. He did idolize his grandfather, whom he referred to as "Emperor Wilhelm the Great."

At twenty-one, he was allowed to join the First Regiment of Foot Guards and begin his military career. For the rest of his life, he would rarely be seen out of uniform. In 1881, he married Princess Augusta Victoria of Schleswig-Holstein, known as "Dona," with whom he would have seven children. The marriage was happy, and Augusta Victoria would prove a devoted, conservative influence throughout his reign.

As crown prince, Wilhelm undertook various diplomatic missions with mixed results, often demonstrating the impulsiveness and tactlessness that would characterize his reign. In 1886, he traveled to Russia to attend the wedding of his cousin, Grand Duke Paul. His meeting with Tsarevich Nicholas (the future Tsar Nicholas II) went poorly. Wilhelm lectured the younger Nicholas on military matters and reportedly behaved in an overbearing manner that offended the Russian court. The incident foreshadowed the personal tensions that would complicate Russo-German relations in the coming decades.

Wilhelm spent much of the 1880s frustrated by his lack of real power and grew increasingly at odds with his liberal parents, particularly over their Anglophile sympathies. He gravitated toward conservative military circles and became known in Berlin for his brash opinions and desire to see Germany assert itself more forcefully in European affairs. In 1888, after the death of his grandfather and then his father, he became the German emperor and king of Prussia at the age of twenty-nine.

Wilhelm II.[19]

Wilhelm II had admired Bismarck for a time, but as emperor, he opposed Bismarck's careful foreign policy and desired for Germany to grow in power and influence. Wilhelm did not like Bismarck's control over the government, as he felt his job as monarch was not just to reign but also to rule his empire.

The break between Wilhelm and the "Iron Chancellor" came after repeated disagreements concerning a series of anti-socialist laws that Bismarck had supported. Bismarck had pushed these laws through in the 1870s to suppress the growing Social Democratic Party, banning socialist organizations and publications. Wilhelm, however, wanted to let the laws expire, believing a softer approach toward workers would better serve the empire. The emperor also showed sympathy toward workers' associations, which the chancellor opposed. Bismarck's Kartell, a political coalition between the German Conservative Party and the National Liberal Party, lost its majority in Parliament. Bismarck, who had spent much of the 1870s waging the Kulturkampf—a bitter political campaign to reduce the Catholic Church's influence over education and civil affairs—had seen that struggle end in failure. His anti-Catholic laws had only unified and strengthened the Catholic Center Party rather than weakening it. By the mid-1880s, Bismarck had quietly rolled back most of the Kulturkampf legislation. Now, he needed votes in the Reichstag, so he attempted negotiations with the very Catholic Center Party he had once tried to destroy. This reversal angered the emperor.

After a heated argument at Bismarck's estate, the chancellor wrote a letter of resignation and left the German government. Bismarck had been, for better or worse, steering the course of Germany since unification, and now, the Kaiser (the emperor) took control. Bismarck apologists argue that Wilhelm's "New Course" was the beginning of the end for the stability of the German Empire. They say that Bismarck's forced resignation set the stage for the collapse of the empire and Prussia, as well as the carnage of the world wars. It is hard to pinpoint a single moment as the root of such earth-shattering events, but Bismarck's departure certainly changed the direction of Germany's policies.

Others argue that Bismarck's dismissal was long overdue. He had alienated almost every faction within Germany at one time or another in the search for scapegoats. Matters outside Germany also played a large role in shaping what the next century would bring. Bismarck was certainly a great statesman, but he was also an aging representative of a generation that needed to step aside and allow the next generation to take its place. He died in 1898, at eighty-three years of age.

Kaiser Wilhelm initially focused on domestic affairs, primarily the protection of workers' rights. However, by the turn of the 20th century, he was looking into foreign matters more closely. He began to build a German navy that, he hoped, would rival the British navy and set Germany up as a world power.

It was around this time that his personality was most noticeable to observers. He was intelligent and forceful but also restless and lacking in dedication. Bismarck had said that the Kaiser wanted every day to be his birthday. Many found him to have unrealistic ideas and to be ignorant of the real world. He believed in social Darwinist ideas like "survival of the fittest" and was often seen as unstable, romantic, erratic, and highly insecure.

He was a first cousin of George V, King of Britain, and he admired the British even though he also hated them. His other royal relatives included Queen Maud of Norway, Queen Victoria Eugenie of Spain, Queen Marie of Romania, and Tsar Nicholas II of Russia. He desperately wanted the approval and attention of his grandmother, Victoria, but he despised his uncle, Bertie, who became King Edward VII upon the death of his mother. He attended both Victoria's funeral in 1901 and Bertie's funeral in 1910. In 1913, he hosted his daughter's wedding. Both King George V and Tsar Nicholas II were in attendance.

The Kaiser came to see Japan as a serious threat to Europe, especially after the Russo-Japanese War. During the Boxer Rebellion in China, he gave a speech to departing German soldiers that included racist imagery and a call to fight like the Huns, giving no quarter. The term "Hun" would later be used by Allied troops in anti-German propaganda.

Wilhelm visited the Ottoman Empire, where he showed support for Sultan Abdul Hamid II. In 1905, he traveled to Tangier, Morocco, where he delivered a provocative speech declaring German support for Moroccan independence and Sultan Abdelaziz, directly challenging French plans to establish a protectorate in Morocco. His actions sparked the First Moroccan Crisis, bringing Europe to the brink of war. An international conference at Algeciras in 1906 largely sided with France, humiliating Germany and heightening international tensions. The crisis demonstrated the dangers of Wilhelm's impulsive diplomacy.

In 1908, Wilhelm gave an interview to *The Daily Telegraph*, a British publication, that proved disastrous. In the interview, he made a series of tactless remarks, including claiming that the English were "mad" and that most Germans were anti-British while insisting he personally was England's friend. He also claimed credit for helping Britain win the Boer War and made provocative comments about Japan and Russia. The interview caused outrage not just in Britain but across Europe and within Germany itself. The Reichstag criticized the emperor, and even his own government condemned his indiscretion. This event severely damaged his political reputation, and he became increasingly withdrawn from public life.

Then, in June of 1914, Archduke Franz Ferdinand of Austria, heir to the Austro-Hungarian throne, was assassinated in Sarajevo by a Serbian nationalist. The aging emperor of Austria, Franz Joseph I, saw an opportunity to crush Serbia, which Austria blamed for fostering nationalist movements that threatened the empire. Austria-Hungary issued an ultimatum to Serbia on July 23rd, with terms deliberately designed to be unacceptable. Serbia accepted most terms but rejected those that would violate its sovereignty. On July 28th, Austria-Hungary declared war on Serbia.

The European alliance system pulled the great powers into the war. Russia, bound by a treaty to protect fellow Slavs in Serbia, began mobilizing its massive army on July 30th. Germany, Austria-Hungary's ally, faced a strategic dilemma. German war planning, embodied in the Schlieffen Plan, assumed Germany would have to fight both Russia and France simultaneously. The plan called for a rapid knockout blow against France through Belgium before Russia could fully mobilize and then shift the forces east to face the Russians. Once Russia began mobilizing, Germany felt compelled to act. Germany declared war on Russia on August 1st, 1914, and on France two days later, on August 3rd.

The German invasion of neutral Belgium on August 4th brought Britain into the war. Britain had guaranteed Belgian neutrality by treaty, and the German violation of that neutrality, which was dismissed by German Chancellor Bethmann Hollweg as a "scrap of paper," gave Britain both a legal obligation and a strategic imperative to intervene. What began as a regional Balkan crisis had exploded into a continental war. It would soon become a world war.

Wilhelm became less and less involved in the government and the actual events of the war. He was increasingly relegated to ceremonial duties and public morale-boosting appearances. The real head of the government was Theobald von Bethmann Hollweg, who served as chancellor from 1909 to 1917. The war that many had predicted would be "over by Christmas" dragged on for years, bogging down into brutal trench warfare on the Western Front. German morale suffered greatly as casualties mounted, and the Allied naval blockade created severe food and material shortages at home.

By 1916, Germany had effectively come under military rule. Field Marshal Paul von Hindenburg, the hero of the Eastern Front, was appointed chief of the General Staff, with General Erich Ludendorff as his deputy. Together, Hindenburg and Ludendorff established what became known as the "Silent Dictatorship," sidelining civilian leadership and making all major strategic decisions. Bethmann Hollweg was eventually forced out in 1917 due to conflicts with the military leadership over war aims and his more moderate policies. Hindenburg and Ludendorff pushed for unrestricted submarine warfare. They wanted to sink ships without warning, including neutral vessels, which outraged the United States.

In January 1917, British intelligence intercepted and decoded a telegram from German Foreign Secretary Arthur Zimmermann to the German ambassador in Mexico. The telegram proposed a military alliance. If the United States entered the war, Germany would support Mexico in reconquering Texas, New Mexico, and Arizona. These territories had been lost to the United States in the 19th century. Britain shared the decoded telegram with the American government, and when it was published in American newspapers in March 1917, public fury erupted. The combination of unrestricted submarine warfare and the Zimmermann Telegram's brazen attempt to incite war on American soil made US entry into the war inevitable. The United States declared war on Germany in April 1917.

With Russia's exit from the war due to the Bolshevik Revolution of 1917, Germany transferred hundreds of thousands of troops from the Eastern Front and launched massive offensives in the spring of 1918. Some hoped these final gambles would bring victory, but the offensives soon stalled. By September of that year, both sides were almost completely exhausted. The arrival of fresh American troops on the Allied side—ten thousand per day by the summer of 1918—sealed Germany's fate. The German Army began to collapse, and Ludendorff demanded that the government seek an armistice.

Germany was thrown into chaos during the revolution of 1918-1919, also known as the "November Revolution." In late October 1918, with defeat imminent, German sailors at Kiel mutinied when ordered to make a final suicidal sortie against the British fleet. The mutiny spread rapidly to other ports and cities. Workers' and soldiers' councils formed across Germany, echoing the Russian Revolution. By early November, the revolution had reached Munich, where a republic was declared, and then Berlin itself.

On November 9th, 1918, mass demonstrations erupted in the capital. The German Empire was dissolving, and Kaiser Wilhelm recognized he would have to give up the imperial crown. He hoped to retain the

Kingdom of Prussia, but the German constitution had tied the empire and Prussia together. This meant that if he abdicated one, he was abdicating the other.

His abdication was announced by the last chancellor of the German Empire, Prince Maximilian of Baden, without the Kaiser's knowledge, but there was little Wilhelm could do. The Socialist Workers' Party, which had taken control, declared Germany a republic. In the end, the military and even diehard royalists like Paul von Hindenburg abandoned the cause of restoring the throne. Wilhelm belatedly released his formal abdication of both thrones on November 28th, officially ending the five-hundred-year reign of the House of Hohenzollern in Prussia.

Wilhelm fled to the Netherlands on November 10th, 1918, just one day before the armistice ended the fighting. The Dutch government granted him asylum despite Allied demands for his extradition to face trial as a war criminal for his role in starting the war. He purchased Huis Doorn, a manor house near Utrecht, where he lived in exile for the remaining twenty-three years of his life. He spent his time chopping wood, studying archaeology, hosting visitors, and writing his memoirs in which he blamed everyone but himself for Germany's defeat. He maintained that he had been betrayed by socialists, Jews, and disloyal generals. This "stab-in-the-back" myth would poison Weimar politics.

Wilhelm lived long enough to see Adolf Hitler come to power. He initially expressed some support for the Nazi restoration of German military strength but grew disillusioned with Hitler's radicalism and vulgarity. When the Netherlands was invaded and occupied by Nazi Germany in 1940, Wilhelm refused Hitler's offer of protection and remained at Huis Doorn. He died there on June 4th, 1941, during the Nazi occupation, having lived to see a second and even more catastrophic world war engulf Germany and Europe. Hitler allowed him a small military funeral, but he forbade Nazi officials from attending. Wilhelm was buried in a mausoleum at Huis Doorn, where he remains to this day.

The new republic, later called the Weimar Republic, was home to the large Free State of Prussia. This was the successor of the Kingdom of Prussia. The leading figure and minister president from 1920 to 1932, excluding two brief interruptions, was Otto Braun. Braun was able to keep Prussia fairly stable, which was not true for the rest of Germany. Prussia remained largely industrial, and unemployment was fairly low. Otto Braun was successful in settling with the House of Hohenzollern over the former royal family's possessions. The Hohenzollerns received large landholdings and financial compensation (reportedly about fifteen million Reichsmarks), while the state kept the royal palaces, parts of the estates, the coronation regalia, works of art, the royal library, and the royal theater. Still, Prussia was not immune to the escalating radicalization on both the left and the right. Conflicts broke out between Communists, Social Democrats, National Socialists, and the police, specifically in Berlin.

Prussia had a particularly strong police force. While the commanders were from varied backgrounds, the officers were mostly ex-soldiers who saw the enemy primarily as Communists and the left. When the Berlin police banned traditional May Day demonstrations in 1929, Communists defied the order and took to the streets. Police opened fire on demonstrators in working-class neighborhoods like Wedding and Neukölln. "Bloody May" ended with 33 dead (mostly civilians), around 200 injured, and more than 1,200 arrested. The Communist Party (KPD) believed the problem was with the Social Democratic Party (SPD), which they saw as the main enemy. The KPD was accused of planning to overthrow the government, which could not be proved. The National Socialists or Nazi Party (NSDAP) saw the other parties as the problem. Joseph Goebbels, the Nazi Party's chief propagandist and leader in Berlin, declared that getting control of Prussia was the key to controlling Germany.

The Prussian government, specifically Otto Braun and his followers, actively opposed Adolf Hitler and the rise of the Nazis. The Prussian authorities monitored Nazi activities closely and gathered evidence of unconstitutional behavior, which they presented to the national government, but it was too little, too late. The NSDAP became the largest party in the Prussian Parliament in the April 1932 election, though it did not have a majority.

On July 20th, 1932, the national government under Chancellor Franz von Papen used Article 48, the emergency powers provision of the Weimar Constitution, to depose the elected Prussian government in what became known as the Preußenschlag ("Prussian Coup"). Papen claimed Prussia could no longer maintain order after clashes between Nazis and Communists, though this was largely a pretext. He appointed himself Reich Commissioner for Prussia, removing Braun and the SPD-led government from power. Otto Braun and the SPD leadership considered armed resistance using the Prussian police, but they ultimately decided against it, fearing such action would trigger a civil war and provide an excuse for even harsher repression. This bloodless coup removed the last major democratic bulwark against Nazi power. With Prussia, which made up nearly two-thirds of Germany's territory and population, now under authoritarian national control, the Weimar Republic's days were numbered.

When Hitler became chancellor in January 1933, Hermann Göring was appointed Reich Commissioner of the Interior for Prussia in February. Göring immediately purged the Prussian civil service and police. Political undesirables, particularly supporters of Braun and the SPD, were systematically removed and replaced with Nazi Party members. The Prussian police became a major instrument in enforcing Nazi rule. The Gestapo, the Nazi secret police force, grew out of the Prussian police under Göring's direction.

The formal end of Prussian autonomy came quickly. Without the votes to secure a majority, the NSDAP used political manipulation to remove and, in many cases, arrest opposing politicians and then secure an absolute majority in the newly formed Nazi-controlled parliament. The Prussian Parliament essentially dissolved in October 1933. In January 1934, the Law on the Reconstruction of the Reich abolished Prussia's administrative autonomy entirely. From that point forward, Prussia existed only as a geographic designation with no real governmental power. The Prussian administration was stripped down, leaving Göring with most of the authority. Hitler himself exercised ultimate control over Prussia through the centralization of power. This structure remained for over a decade until the end of World War II and Nazi Germany's defeat at the hands of the Allied Powers.

Germany was divided into occupation zones, and almost everything east of the Oder-Neisse Line—roughly one-quarter of pre-war German territory—became part of Poland. Most of this lost territory had been Prussia's historic heartland: Pomerania, Silesia, Brandenburg east of the Oder, and most of East and West Prussia. The northern third of East Prussia became Soviet territory. The ancient city of Königsberg was renamed Kaliningrad, and the region became the Kaliningrad Oblast, a Russian enclave between Lithuania and Poland. This area remains part of Russia to this day.

Between 1945 and 1950, an estimated twelve to fourteen million Germans fled or were forcibly expelled from former Prussian and other eastern German territories now under Polish and Soviet control.

Hundreds of thousands died during the expulsions from exposure, starvation, and violence. Russians, Poles, and Ukrainians were resettled in these emptied territories, completely transforming the region's demographics.

The Control Council Law No. 46, signed February 25th, 1947, officially dissolved Prussia as a legal and political entity. The Allied Control Council declared that Prussia, "which from early days has been a bearer of militarism and reaction in Germany," had ceased to exist. The remaining Prussian territories in western Germany were divided into smaller states, which are today part of the unified Germany. Of the current sixteen states of Germany, none carries the name Prussia. After the war, Berlin was divided between East and West and featured the famous wall bearing its name. Berlin, which was once the capital of the Prussian state, is now the capital of the nation of Germany.

Conclusion

While Prussia has largely faded from most of the world's memory, it is still certainly remembered in Germany and the areas that were once a part of this remarkable nation. Prussia's legacy is complex and hard to place in the modern world, but it is there regardless. Many today might only recognize the name as it relates to the famous "Prussian Blue" or "Berlin Blue," a synthetic pigment of a deep blue color that was most likely first created in the early 18th century by paint maker Johann Jacob Diesbach in Berlin. Others may think of Prussians as a military-centered culture known for battling Napoleon, Austria, Russia, and many other European powers. What is perhaps lost is that the Prussians were artists, businessmen, and philosophers as well.

Great, dynamic, and controversial characters have played major roles in Prussian history, from outsiders like Voltaire, who influenced Frederick the Great's intellectual life, to native Prussians like Immanuel Kant and Frederick the Great. From the early medieval beginnings of the Old Prussians and then the Teutonic Knights to the German unification orchestrated by the Iron Chancellor, Prussia has played a key role in European and global history. The history of Prussia is so closely intertwined with that of Germany that the two are inseparable. One cannot talk about modern Germany without mentioning how the national colors of black, red, and gold were associated with German volunteers during the wars against Napoleon, many of whom served under Prussian command, or how Otto von Bismarck came to define Germany and how Kaiser Wilhelm of the House of Hohenzollern played a role in the outbreak of World War I.

To define modern Germany or even modern Europe, one must look to the history of Prussia to see how the evolution of German identity was formed. It is certainly a story worth telling. At one point, Prussia was a backwater and, by the accident of hereditary titles, came to be connected to the elector of Brandenburg. With that little bit of power, great Prussian leaders leveraged their way from subservience to the Holy Roman emperor to sovereign kings. From there, they spread to control huge swaths of land along the Baltic Sea and down into the German hinterlands. Eventually, the Prussians, descended from a mixture of German, Polish, Lithuanian, and Scandinavian peoples, came to rule a great central European empire that had colonies in Africa and the South Pacific.

The German emperors, all descended from the House of Hohenzollern, which came from Brandenburg and then Prussia, were among the most powerful of Europe's leaders. Where once Prussia had been fearful of Austria, Russia, and France, they began to dominate them in negotiations and political maneuvering. Yet, it was perhaps that great ambition of the Prussian people that led to their eventual downfall in the First World War. Still, the state of Prussia carried on, although it could not stop the rise of the Nazi Party and the eventual destruction of the state after the end of the Second World War.

Prussia no longer exists. It cannot be picked out on a map. The pieces that once made the whole are spread between different nations, and none carry the once powerful name of Prussia as a state, though the name survives in cultural and historical institutions. Yet, the legacy and the lessons that Prussia has to give remain as strong as ever. The cities of Prussia remain, many as great as ever. The palaces of its kings still stand. However, these are not the things that carry on Prussia's legacy. Rather, it is the story of the rise and fall of one of the most extraordinary powers of the world that will keep Prussia alive in the centuries to come.

Here's another book by Enthralling History that you might like

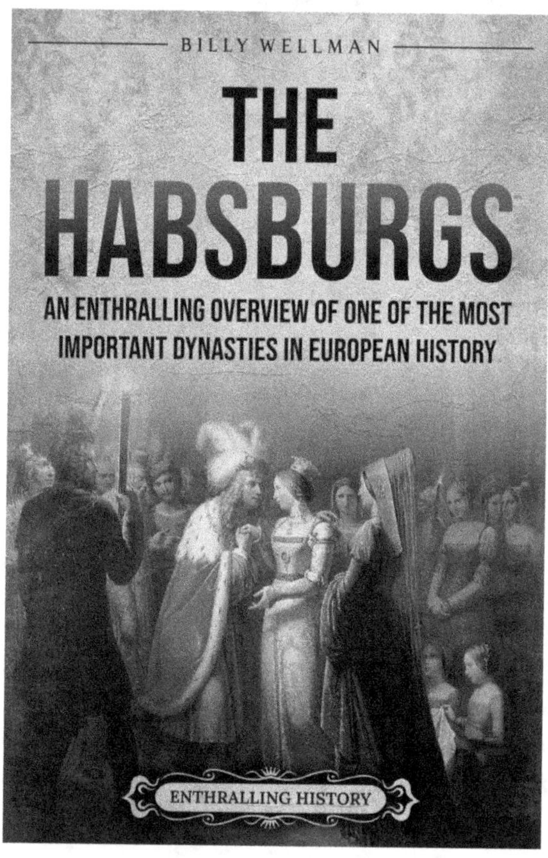

Free limited time bonus

Stop for a moment. We have a free bonus set up for you. The problem is this: we forget 90% of everything that we read after 7 days. Crazy fact, right? Here's the solution: we've created a printable, 1-page pdf summary for this book that you're reading now. All you have to do to get your free pdf summary is to go to the following website:

https://livetolearn.lpages.co/enthrallinghistory/

Or, Scan the QR code!

Once you do, it will be intuitive. Enjoy, and thank you!

Bibliography

Bach, Thomas Parnell. "Throne and Altar: Pietism and the Hohenzollerns." PhD diss., University of South Carolina, 1995.

Clark, Christopher. *Iron Kingdom: The Rise and Downfall of Prussia, 1600–1947.* Cambridge, MA: Belknap Press of Harvard University Press, 2006.

Colla, Marcus. "Constructing the Prussia-Myth in East Germany, 1945–61." *Journal of Contemporary History* 54, no. 3 (2019): 557–581.

Duffy, Christopher. *The Army of Frederick the Great.* New York: Hippocrene Books, 1974.

Dwyer, Philip G., ed. *Modern Prussian History, 1830–1947.* Cambridge: Cambridge University Press, 2014.

Friedrich, Karin. *The Other Prussia: Royal Prussia, Poland and Liberty, 1569–1772.* Cambridge: Cambridge University Press, 2000.

Haffner, Sebastian. *The Rise and Fall of Prussia.* Translated by Terence Prittie. London: Weidenfeld & Nicolson, 1981.

Jeroschin, Nikolaus von. *The Chronicle of Prussia.* Translated and edited by Mary Fischer. Farnham: Ashgate, 2012.

Koch, H. W. *A History of Prussia.* London: Longman, 1978.

McKay, Derek. The Great Elector: Frederick William of Brandenburg-Prussia. London: Longman, 2001.

Murray, Scott W. "The Origins of an Illusion: British Policy and Opinion, and the Development of Prussian Liberalism, 1848–1871." PhD diss., University of Oxford, 2004.

Shennan, Margaret. *The Rise of Brandenburg-Prussia 1618–1740.* London: Routledge, 1995.

Image Sources

1 MapMaster, CC BY-SA 3.0 <http://creativecommons.org/licenses/by-sa/3.0/>, via Wikimedia Commons, https://commons.wikimedia.org /wiki/File:Baltic_Tribes_c_1200.svg

2 S. Bollmann, CC BY-SA 3.0 <https://creativecommons.org/licenses/by-sa/3.0>, via Wikimedia Commons, https://commons.wikimedia.org/wiki/File: Teutonic_Order_1410.png

3 https://commons.wikimedia.org/wiki/File:Frans_Luycx_-_Frederick_William,_Elector_of_Brandenburg,_at_three-quarter-length.jpg

4 https://commons.wikimedia.org/wiki/File:Adolph-von-Menzel-Tafelrunde2.jpg

5 https://commons.wikimedia.org/wiki/File:Christian_Wolff.jpg

6 Rijksmuseum, CC0, via Wikimedia Commons, https://commons.wikimedia.org/wiki/File:Portret_van_Pierre_Louis_Maupertuis,_R P-P-1910-4953.jpg

7 https://commons.wikimedia.org/wiki/File:D%27apr%C3%A8s_Nicolas_de_ Largilli%C3%A8re,_portrait_de_Voltaire_(Institut_et_Mus%C3%A9e_Voltaire)_-001.jpg

8 https://commons.wikimedia.org/wiki/File:BachC.P.E-739858.jpg

9 https://commons.wikimedia.org/wiki/File:Jean-Baptiste_de_Boyer_Marquis_d%27Argens.jpg

10 https://commons.wikimedia.org/wiki/File:Portrait_de_Julien_Offray_de_La_Mettrie.jpg

11 https://commons.wikimedia.org/wiki/File:Francesco_Algarotti_(Liotard).jpg

12 https://commons.wikimedia.org/wiki/File:Immanuel_Kant_portrait_c1790.jpg

13 Bryan Rutherford, CC BY-SA 4.0 <https://creativecommons.org/licenses/by-sa/4.0>, via Wikimedia Commons, https://commons.wikimedia.org/wiki/File: Europe_1740_en.png

14 Bryan Rutherford, CC BY-SA 4.0 <https://creativecommons.org/licenses/by-sa/4.0>, via Wikimedia Commons, https://commons.wikimedia.org/wiki/File:Europe_1783-1792_en.png

15 https://commons.wikimedia.org/wiki/File:Antoine_Pesne_-_Frederick_the_Great_as_Crown_Prince_-_WGA17377.jpg

16 Arthur Kampf, CC BY-SA 4.0 <https://creativecommons.org/licenses/by-sa/4.0>, via Wikimedia Commons, https://commons.wikimedia.org/wiki/File: Frederick_the_Great_as_standard-bearer_at_the_battlefield.jpg

17 Thomas Wolf, www.foto-tw.de, CC BY-SA 3.0 <https://creativecommons.org/licenses/by-sa/3.0>, via Wikimedia Commons, https://commons.wikimedia.org/wiki/File:Brandenburger_Tor_abends.jpg

18 https://commons.wikimedia.org/wiki/File:Bust_of_Queen_Louise_asleep,_by_Christian_Daniel_Rauch,_1817,_marble_-_Germanisches_Nationalmuseum_-_Nuremberg,_Germany_-_DSC03377.jpg

19 https://commons.wikimedia.org/wiki/File:Kaiser_Wilhelm_II_of_Germany_-_1902_(cropped).jpg